POLITICIANS
and Other Scoundrels

POLITICIANS
and Other Scoundrels

Being a fulsome compendium of observations, mostly disenchanted
and dyspeptic,
About politics and politicians and their
Arcane doings down through the
Ages, from time immemorial

To the present, with
Sufficient attention
To the
United States of America
(A glorious land of liberty),

All introduced, with the enlightening comments of a mordant

FOREWORD
Supplied by their compiler, Ferdinand Lundberg,
Who as a writer is esteemed by some of the more perspicacious,
Scorned by a churlish few,
Indifferently received by many
And ignored by God's own vast multitude.

This book is solemnly dedicated to the learned societies of the
world.

LYLE STUART INC.　　●　　SECAUCUS, N. J.

Published by Lyle Stuart Inc.
120 Enterprise Avenue, Secaucus, N.J. 07094
In Canada: Musson Book Company
A division of General Publishing Co. Limited
Don Mills, Ontario

First published under the title *Scoundrels All*

Manufactured in the United States of America
ISBN 0-8184-0483-3

To Lyndon Baines Johnson, hailed on every
hand as the master politician
of our day

Preface

STRANGER: Therefore all who take part in one of these
governments [monarchic or tyrannic, aristocratic or
oligarchic, direct democratic or representative]—
apart from the one based on real knowledge—are to
be distinguished from the true statesman. They are
not statesmen; they are party leaders, leaders of bogus
governments and themselves as bogus as their systems.
The supreme imitators and tricksters, they are of all
Sophists the arch-Sophists.
YOUNG SOCRATES: It seems to me that the wheel
has come full circle, now that the title of Sophist goes

to those who most deserve it, to the men who get themselves called political leaders.

STRANGER: So this fantastic pageant that seemed like some strange masque of centaurs or some band of satyrs stands revealed for what it is. At much pains we have succeeded at last in distinguishing them and setting them apart, as we must, from all true practice of statesmanship.

PLATO: *Statesman* (trans. by J. B. Skemp)

STRANGER: I will, and I can clearly make out a pair of them. I see one who can keep up his dissimulation publicly in long speeches to a large assembly. The other uses short arguments in private and forces others to contradict themselves in conversation.

THEAETETUS: Very true.

STRANGER: And with whom shall we identify the more long-winded type—with the statesman or with the demagogue?

THEAETETUS: The demagogue.

STRANGER: And what shall we call the other—wise man or Sophist?

THEAETETUS: We cannot surely call him wise, because we set him down as ignorant, but as a mimic of the wise he will clearly assume a title derived from his, and I now see that here at last is the man who must be truly described as the real and genuine Sophist.

STRANGER: Shall we, then, as before collect all the elements of his description, from the end to the beginning, and draw our threads together in a knot?

THEAETETUS: By all means.

STRANGER: The art of contradiction making, de-

10

scended from an insincere kind of conceited mimicry, of the semblance-making breed, derived from image making, distinguished as a portion, not divine but human, of production, that presents a shadow play of words—such are the blood and lineage which can, with perfect truth, be assigned to the authentic Sophist.

THEAETETUS: I entirely agree.

PLATO: *The Sophist* (trans. by F. M. Cornford)

The Crazy World of Politicians and Politics

Politicians, as anyone can see, run the world, and badly, over both the long and the short runs. When affairs become completely chaotic, as they commonly do over a succession of short runs, a new set of politicos emerges to direct the political circus in some climactic caper of long-delayed reform, reaction, or revolution. When this happens it is commonly said, in all seriousness, that history is being made. What goes on over the whole area is as endlessly fascinating as watching a cageful of impish chimpanzees apportioning among themselves a bunch of bananas. In the meantime humanity bleeds and suffers, and dark nu-

13

clear prospects loom ahead—all part of what is a farce on the surface, a tragedy underneath.

Consequently it is not strange that politicians and their politics down through the centuries have been given close attention by sharp-witted commentators, as numerous as they are of divergent outlook. On one thing they all seem agreed: Politicians are pretty uniformly of a dubious breed. It is the purpose of this book to give an extensive sampling of such remarks of record, not a few of them never before recorded in any collection laid before polite readers. My intention is frankly to be, if possible, diverting rather than instructive, for which reason I shall give special attention to the United States, a country that has been made by its politicians into something comical in a sadly elephantine way.

A common note down through the centuries in the comments about politicians and politics is that of reprehension and rejection of all their works. This note was first sounded on the record by Plato, so that from near the very beginning of western civilization it has had impressive sponsorship. Not a few of the more candid practitioners of the black art themselves have joined from time to time in the chorus. The politician, indeed, like the prostitute, is universally condemned even as he is freely resorted to. Yet, unlike the prostitute, he at times manages to draw upon himself extravagant honor, especially when he is deemed (usually erroneously) to have, like Moses, saved his constituents from some enveloping calamity. In the end he saves nobody, as shown by the uniform eventual demise of civilizations and nation-states, a clearly avoidable sequel. No doubt, like the bedraggled sisterhood of dubious joy, he does something (if only psychic) to fill a formally necessary

14

role in the tangled lives of nations, although calamity eventually engulfs them all as a consequence of fumbles by political leaders. While it is true that there is a role here to be well played, the question is: Does the common politician satisfy the demands of the role?

Why the politician should be so often condemned, so seldom praised, is not difficult to discern in some of his roles, but in others the reasons for his unpopularity are more elusive and, possibly, instructive. For there is a lugubrious sort of instruction to be gained from this frequently obscene spectacle.

II

In broadest generality, whenever a politician makes a decision—right or wrong, good or bad, corrupt or honorable—he makes enemies. And some of his enemies have been acidly articulate. Nobody has ever said anything on behalf of the politician half so sharp and true as many intelligent men have said against him. Nor has any politician succeeded in producing a plausible apologia of his own for the breed. It is, then, part of his occupational hazard that he have enemies. Yet even his friends, as in the case of the prostitute, fail to praise him. Even when he is grossly calumniated, nobody of stature rises to defend him. What I term the politician is anyone commonly regarded as such who figures at one level or another of political rule from precinct or cell captain to party chairman or even chief officeholder of the nation. President Lyndon B. Johnson while in office was commonly presented by the press as a typical adroit American politician, a very model of a grassroots, sweating, down-to-earth practitioner.

As we scan the world we note that politicians hold their places (whatever they may be) through election, cooptation by some dominating party, or through the seizure of office by force as in Greece recently. Their rise by the first two methods is usually the end-consequence of nothing more than protracted weasel-like intrigue, this accounting for often placing extremely grotesque types in high offices. All regimes are established, recently or more remotely, by brute force, nothing less.

Being actually rulers, overt or covert, politicians wield power under established authority, *de facto* or *de jure*. And it is as authoritarian power-wielders, decision-makers, that they encounter their first critics. As George Washington said, "Government is not reason, it is not eloquence—it is force." Hence the large number of generals in political power all over the world.

While most people seem happy to bend to authority when it is reasonably applied as a necessary requisite to order, not everyone feels this way, as the hard-core penal population shows. Again, politicians are not held to account because they have properly or reasonably used authority; it is repeatedly charged and disclosed that they have abused it for their own short-term advantage or out of simple ignorance.

III

Not only is the politician in authority, or about to assume it, but he is commonly a relatively ignorant man, often an obvious oaf. Confining oneself entirely to the highest places one could produce a short list here of presumably learned politicians thoroughly ignorant even in spheres in which

16

they were partaking in important decisions. Although he occupies positions for which one would suppose only the highest and most diversified skills were necessary, he usually possesses none at all beyond the ability to attain and retain office (up to the point where he is dismissed by events). The procession of ignorant Hitlers, Mussolinis, Tojos, Chiang Kai-sheks, Stalins, Sukarnos, and Nassers, bunglers from start to finish, is long in world history; and millions of dead lie in their wake. In a lamentable case nearer home there was, of course, Neville Chamberlain, as inept in his role as anyone could possibly be. And as was Stanley Baldwin before him, and Ramsay MacDonald before him, and . . . and . . . and . . . . The British Empire, an accident of construction, in point of fact, was gradually liquidated by a long line of obtuse John Bullish politicians. More recently we have had another example of devious ineptitude in Lyndon B. Johnson, the wild man from Texas who unsolicitedly dedicated himself to saving the United States at disproportionate expense from the distant savage bands of Ho Chi Minh, a bush-league politico. In the attempt to do this Johnson, going back on his publicly pledged word not to, threw the economy of the United States far out of kilter and stirred up dark social currents that will be long in subsiding. He sought, in fact, to kill a mosquito with an artillery barrage. By 1968 it looked as though Johnson, hailed as a typical politician, would go down in history as the worst president the United States ever had, rating even below Grant and Harding in a long procession of nincompoops.

Most politicians do not know anything whatever, special or general, that the world counts as knowledge. It was a topic of wide, incredulous, and repeated remark that John

F. Kennedy was an omnivorous and rapid reader, a talent that nobody expected to find in a politician. He was, to boot, a writer and, oddly, the holder of a first-class university diploma. What could one be sure Lyndon B. Johnson knew other than the technique of *sub rosa* intrigue, indirect and sinister? And Johnson, except for his self-assertion, was always pretty typical among professional American politicians, spiritually on a par with Harding and Coolidge, Buchanan and Hayes. Without an erudite secretary or a trained research staff in the background, most of the very highest politicians would more quickly than customary reveal themselves as hollow jugs, fugitives from knowledge even of statecraft. If one were to draw up a list of full-time American politicians whose mental reach encompassed anything more than an encyclopedia of misinformation and outworn maxims, one would surely come close to naming 90 per cent of them.

The insight that most politicians do not know anything, and know in particular nothing relevant to running their government safely and effectively, was achieved at least as long ago as the fourth century, B.C., by Plato, who had many disparaging things to say about the political ilk of his day. His remedy was to visualize a government the offices of which were open exclusively to men of knowledge, a notion ever afterward immoderately derided by the herd and its tribunes much as were once the notions that the earth was round and revolved around the sun. Some latter-day observers appear to believe that Plato's prescription has in effect been met by the practice of having men of special knowledge and civil servants function as subordinates and special advisers to politicians; but as the latter always retain the veto power over the rational application of special knowledge—and use it freely—there has clearly not been much advance. Most politicians commonly veto better minds.

That most persons who attain political office do not know much beyond ways of insinuating and ingratiating themselves among ordinary men is a proposition easily supported with respect to any period of history, and of present times most conspicuously and particularly with respect to the more advanced and large countries. The smaller advanced countries, no doubt feeling some justified apprehension about their safety in the presence of the predatory giants, appear to have come around to selecting more reliable types, almost technicians, as political leaders. They seem to feel they cannot afford the sort of free-wheeling corruption and incompetence so blatantly evident in the United States, Latin America, India, the Middle East, Africa, and China. Corruption, I agree, may be present elsewhere, but the operative words in what I said are "so evident." My reference to small countries, of course, relates to Scandinavia, Switzerland, Holland, Belgium, and, perhaps, Japan.

A list of all the politicians in the world who had even an elementary grasp of any identifiable body of knowledge would be a short one. And the list of generalists in knowledge among them would be even shorter. What I have in mind here is someone like Paul Painlevé (1863-1933), a mathematician who filled various high public posts and eventually became premier of France. Even while serving in government Painlevé taught at the Sorbonne. Not that knowing mathematics necessarily made Painlevé a better national leader, but it at least showed him capable of knowing something solid, which is more than we can be

19

sure of in the case of most politicians. What is most notable about them is their inability to learn, their clinging to outworn rules of thumb. It is in the blind application of these simple rules of thumb to crucial affairs of state that disaster often ensues, like American entanglement in Vietnam. If a plumber knew as little of his craft as does the average high politician, mankind would long ago have been drowned in sewage, as indeed it is currently being drowned in political sewage.

"After talking to world leaders for years I am really appalled at how few people have the answers," said the late Hugh Baillie, from 1935 to 1955 president of the United Press Association and a great believer in gadding about sounding for the emaciated opinions of political VIPs. "It gives you a 'gone' feeling to realize that leaders have no more answers than you do" (*New York Times,* March 2, 1966; 41:2).

Baillie's was a common experience the world over of intelligent newspaper men. They at last sadly realize that most of the men they talk to are boobs and, when a Kennedy, Roosevelt II, or Churchill comes along, so happy are they that they throw off all critical restraint and present an above-average operator as a colossal sage, an Einstein of statesmanship.

Scientists as well as philosophers, the ancient Greek version of the modern scientist, are unheard of among politicos. Often cited as a man of knowledge in American politics of the past one hundred and fifty years is Woodrow Wilson, a simple-minded professor of jurisprudence, next door to a lawyer, with the members of which profession politics abounds. While there are broadly knowledgeable lawyers, true generalists, made knowledgeable on their own extracurricular account, a lawyer merely as such is no more a man of learning than was the ancient barber-surgeon. Wilson can hardly count as a man of more than provincial knowledge, cannot be cited (as he sometimes is) as exemplifying the danger of trusting a man of authentic knowledge in high office. The argument, often heard, against having men of certified knowledge in office must rest on the queer presupposition that there are situations wherein lack of knowledge is better than knowledge.

IV

What is clearly the case, and what makes politics so very difficult in the attainment of satisfactory outcomes, is—as a mathematician would say—that the political situation always consists of a multiplicity of present and future variables—too many for any man with known methods to take judicious account of. Moreover, each of these variables is of unknown or different weight and often of changing weight from time to time. There remains, too, the question of priorities among the variables. Politicians generally give higher priority to war and preparing for war than in establishing internal distributive justice, finding it easier to subdue foolish domestic populations with fancy words than cagy and even insane foreign rivals, which need to be coerced with heavy weapons and armies. Although they easily deceive the broad public, politicians do not easily deceive each other. They know what their opposite numbers are after.

Even with the utmost knowledge, probity, and self-conscious limitation of personal prejudice and self-oriented interest, a political practitioner would have the utmost

21

difficulty mastering the situation: For politics properly pursued is far from simple, is indeed far more complex than advanced calculus. One must remember, too, that even as the politician may be trying to master his situation in a systematic way on a high level of performance, as a mathematician tries to master a complex problem, there are power-seeking rivals all about him pulling the rug from under his feet, jogging his elbow, uttering wild cat-calls, and doing their best to frighten the public about his intentions. The serious-minded politician's lot is never a happy one, and the sincerely constructive politician is invariably much unhappier than the reckless adventurer who preens himself in imagined superiority.

It is very probably the difficulty of the situation and the lack of sure methods for dealing with it that induce most intelligent men to stay away from politics. What appears to be the case, speculatively, is that men of knowledge have used up their aggressive qualities in acquiring knowledge, the pursuit of which requires a great deal of aggression. Faced by the political problem, their reservoirs of aggressiveness are low, so they turn away, abstain, and are looked upon by the common politico as tabby cats. Such abstention, of course, leaves the field clear for aggressively adventurous, reckless, imprudent, and unscrupulous hacks, bluffers, and braggarts, all armored with the presumption of a demented rhinoceros, to move in, take over and seek uninformed applause for brilliant strokes of ineptitude. There can be no doubt that consistently low, untutored types, fit only for treasons, spoils, and stratagems, dominate the politics of nearly every country, particularly in the more powerful developed countries but also in the undeveloped countries. For the greater the power available, especially in the absence of firm institutional tradition, the more ruthless the claimants to it.

V

To top all this off, many persons in politics, especially on the very highest levels, are plainly mentally disordered, 4-11 alarms as far as psychiatrists are concerned. While by no means true of all, politicians as a group obviously comprise a greater proportion of social misfits than any other occupation except prostitutes. One could run off a long list of political incumbents who by every criterion known to psychiatry and ordinary horse sense classify as highly disturbed mentally. Many psychiatrists have made pointed note of the fact, observing especially how pathological bellicosity easily masquerades as intense patriotism.

The world, without referring at all to Hitler, Stalin, Mussolini, Tojo, or any other standard butts, is run in many of its important lethal divisions by men who are far off their rockers. Militant racists, for example, leaders and followers, are by every criterion known to science and psychiatry wildly deviant from ordinary sanity. For there is nothing whatever inherent about being Jewish, Negro, Oriental, Amerindian, Latinic, or polyglot that gives warrant to any rational person for feelings of rising ire. Such feelings are part of mental derangement—always. There isn't an accredited mental doctor who would deny it.

VI

As it is, the prime beneficiaries of so-called practical politics, we must believe, are perfectly content with matters as they stand. They take no remedial steps. They are getting theirs, which is all that seems to concern them. Only the quixotic, having little concretely at stake, undertake even to grumble. What the practical man does about the politician, if he can, is to get him on his side by paying him off in whatever coin he requires. Thereafter he feels he must make the best of any general conditions produced by political ineptitude and irrationality. And if matters get too bad, the offending politicians can sometimes be dumped in favor of more manageable replacements, after which the odious and entirely avoidable process starts over again.

There is, then, never any fundamental change short of revolution, an observation against which the respectable and established will recoil in protest. But even the most respectable indirectly pay their deepest political tribute to revolutionists. We see this in the United States in the tributes fulsomely paid on any and every occasion to the Founding Fathers and their Constitution. What is seldom noticed about such tributes is that the Founding Fathers were all-out revolutionists, shunned and condemned by the respectables of their day; they were men who did not believe any fundamental change was possible without extreme violence. Although they believed as deeply as anyone in law and order, it was a belief in their own version of law and order. They could not have written the Constitution had they not been revolutionists first.

VII

While all this may seem academic to some, it really is not. For it all has a profound bearing on war and peace.

24

In an oft-quoted remark, General Von Clausewitz said that war is politics carried on by other means. Conversely, politics itself is war without military weapons, with military weapons held in reserve. It is domestic and external war, not (as sometimes asserted) mild adjustment of conflicting claims through power brokers.

The politician invariably rules domestically over hordes of people conscious of their insecurity—of position, of property, of advantage, and of those with feelings of utter cosmic insecurity. For the latter, religion has been devised, with the profound blessings of most politicians. For those whose feelings of insecurity stem from more obvious emotional malfunctioning, the psychiatrist has been invented. But for all others the politician functions, his general task being to retain behind the banner of patriotism the advantage for those, his paymasters, that have an advantage over others in whatever particular context one finds him.

As politics itself is devious warfare—of the advantaged against the less advantaged and feebly *vice versa*—the effort of those who would end military warfare by invoking politics must be seen as mistaken. The effort begins at the end of a determining series whereas it should begin at the beginning of the series.

The place to begin if one wishes to end warfare among men, domestic and foreign, is to assuage their feelings of insecurity, from whatever source they may come. Manifestly this is a colossal task, impossible by any presently known method other than by administering tranquilizing drugs to nearly everyone. Politics itself, the nucleus of war, would ideally never be allowed to begin, and there would be no need of politicians. Affairs would be run rationally by hired civil servants, with the public accepting the sensible arrangements these made the way it now accepts arrangements as they find them in a large department store. Nobody would try to overreach anyone else.

To await the onset of the day when governmental affairs are left to highly trained, dedicated civil servants, I admit, would be to wait a long time. Such a day is not in sight, fantasied though it was in Plato's *Republic*.

VIII

In the meantime the politician, for all his ineptitude in the management of public affairs, serves the useful function of scapegoat for the failings of other men in dealing with their own insecurities, genuine and imagined. The reason for the existence of the politician, as of the prostitute, is to be found in the nature of the populace, which contrary to latter-day democratic doctrine is far from uniformly benign.

Indeed, when all the returns are in, it seems pretty certain that the politician is generally a person of a higher cut, no matter who he is, than the average of his constituency, just as the prostitute is often a better person than some of her customers.

Difficult though this may be to believe for those saturated with pseudo-liberal pap (for nothing is liberal that is false), one can see the clear superiority of many political men in many of our jurisdictions. Senator J. William Fulbright is hardly typical of the Arkansas mind; he is, clearly, far above it. The same is manifestly true of Senators Lister Hill and John J. Sparkman of Alabama. The difference between a Senator John Stennis of Mississippi and a large percentage of Mississippians is that between a mastermind and a horde of far-gone morons. And so it is, although less strikingly, in many other American jurisdictions, federal or local. The farther any politician deviates from the universal criteria of seemliness the more is he like a greater proportion of his constituency. Adolf Hitler, for example, resembled the hopes, aspirations, and outlook of far more Germans than did, for example, Bismarck, relatively a superior man. Senator Joseph R. McCarthy, at his worst, spoke and acted on behalf of a wide section of the American public. If anything, McCarthy did not go far enough in their eyes.

That the public which so freely condemns the politician while seeking him out is itself not without blemish has been long recognized, although disoriented latter-day democrats have made it a fashion to ignore such sober observations. Thus, Cicero (106-43 B.C.) remarked: "In the common people there is no wisdom, no penetration, no power of judgment." And Niccolò Machiavelli observed: "The masses of the people resemble a wild beast, which, naturally fierce, and accustomed to live in the woods, has been brought up, as it were, in a prison, and having by accident obtained its liberty, not being accustomed to search for its own good, and not knowing where to hide, easily becomes the prey of the first who seeks to imprison it again." Such acute observations, including Alexander Pope's, "The people are a many-headed beast," if laid end to end would encircle the earth.

Should anyone assume that I am in this matter relying on the word of foreigners, tainted as they are with vile un-Americanism, let us turn to E. W. ("Ed") Howe, celebrated American small-town newspaper editor who lived his life among the common people. As this homespun

American put it in 1911, "One secret has been kept many centuries: the terrible worthlessness of the people collectively." We have here, clearly, a grass-roots evaluation, by one who was of, by, and for the grass roots.

It is hardly difficult, then, to see wherein lies the politician's eternal opportunity. Like the prostitute, he has many potential shabby patrons and supporters. Not that comparison of the politician with the prostitute should be taken by the prudish as indicating on my part any severe reprehension of the dedicated sisterhood. There are, as is well known, what are called high-class prostitutes; not all of the profession consists of common bawds, trollops, and strumpets. And so it is with politicians. Some are several cuts above the others, almost civilized.

But that the role of the politician is usually played on any higher level than that of the common prostitute may be safely denied, whatever the inherently ignoble condition of his constituency. And here we may well cogitate over the testimony of witnesses down through history, which are herein offered concentratedly to the reader.

It is commonly thought nowadays that politicians represent and express the form of existent society. Thus, there are now said to be capitalist politicians, communist politicians, and socialist politicians. However, politicians in their purity are nonideological, employ ideology only because of the susceptibility of the populace to it. What is more nearly the case is that professional politicians do not love their social understructure beyond their special dependence upon it. They are more nearly free-lance parasites upon it than its defenders. This stands clear in the fact that few if any among them seek to alter for the better whatever social understructure they find ready to their hand. In fact, they strongly tend to resist even minor improvements.

This being the case, full-fledged professional politicians could easily function in alien systems with hardly any loss of stride if they were given a supporting staff, including translators. The interchangeability, say, of Richard M. Nixon and Lyndon B. Johnson with Leonid Brezhnev and Aleksei Kosygin seems strikingly apparent. Not only are the two pairs devious do-alikes but, less important though noteworthy, they are very much look-alikes. I have often wondered why some enterprising picture magazine did not take the annual comical line-up of politicos before Lenin's tomb and paste in the faces of leading American politicians. Only when it came to inserting faces such as those of John F. Kennedy, Franklin D. Roosevelt, and Adlai Stevenson would there be any strain on credibility. It was widely remarked during his incumbency that Nikita Khrushchev could well have been an American politician, so vulgarly low-down was his style. He would have made a fairly typical senator from South Carolina—or Illinois.

The troubles of nations obviously trace directly back to the boobishness of some set of politicians. As the people in charge, they are plainly responsible for much that happens, including much for which they are never blamed. For it is in the devious nature of the political game as it is necessarily played to make the practitioners furtive if they were not so to begin with. Natural sneaks, of course, have an obvious advantage over bolder temperaments in the political sweepstakes.

What I mean here can be made clear by citing two salient cases. It was plainly evident more than forty years ago that population growth in the United States was fast outstripping resources and facilities and that millions of families were doomed to permanent poverty by an excess of children. A nurse, Mrs. Margaret Sanger, took it upon herself to alert the public and show a reasonable way of saner practices. Ignored by most politicians, she was brutally jailed by the politicians nearest to her at the behest of self-appointed pseudo-religious ecclesiastical bureaucrats. True, had any politician spoken up on her behalf he would have been destroyed politically in all probability; but politicians expect the young men of the nation to face bravely total destruction by the millions as soon as some colleague takes to blowing the bugle wildly in a gamey cause. Politicians themselves seldom take comparable chances.

The present condition of the Negroes in the United States is wholly the consequence of politicians acquiescing unanimously in the "democratic" demands of the most deranged strata in the populace, failing to take a responsible stand. Not only did the politicians out of sheer cowardice perpetuate the serfdom of the Negroes in the South up to the 1930's but they thereafter made it worse by failing to prepare or even talk about new environments for Negroes. They first acquiesced in the installation of labor-canceling machinery in the South, thus depriving Negroes of meager jobs. They then joined in urging Negroes to move to other areas of the country, presumably to get higher paying jobs. But they made no provision whatever in any region for this vast influx of a new, ill-trained populace. The result was a vast, predictable expansion of slums and proliferation of urban unemployment, adding poor Negroes to impoverished city whites.

It is true that any present set of politicians is always

wrestling with a large accumulation of mistakes and evasions by their predecessors. Nothing is ever solved; old problems are simply absorbed in new problems.

The cure for the pretty universally sorry state of public affairs, of course, lies somewhere within the public. And this perhaps only indicates that it will never be applied. Mankind apparently must go on forever stumbling from disaster to disaster. For no individual or group has yet been able to develop the leverage necessary to alter conditions significantly. Radicals, blaming capitalism, simply move on to establish dictatorial state capitalism and call it communism. By all available signs, the world is doomed to remain under the thumbs of politicians, at least until some ingenious discoverer finds a road to the Platonic Nirvana.

Plato himself never saw any way of placing reflective men of knowledge in charge of affairs of state other than by inducing through rational argument some tyrant to install the method and solidify it by force. But no tyrants, themselves invariably men of herd mentality up from the lower depths, have ever seen fit to implement this Platonic program. Tyrants are as opposed to autonomous men of learning as are the common people.

IX

In conclusion a note on the American politician will not be out of place, since this book is aimed primarily at politically bedeviled American readers.

While politics is mishandled enough in its general historical context, under the hogwash universal franchise as it has developed in the United States there have emerged some particularly grotesque varieties of the political breed,

31

resembling extravagantly monstrous, nightmarish denizens —centaurs, griffins, satyrs, chimeras—surfacing from the ocean depths. To describe some of these unqualified characters in all sobriety is to strain the credulity of anyone who has not encountered them in the flesh.

American public freedom has been hymned for a variety of reasons, but one of the attractive minor reasons for such freedom is that it enables oafish public figures to disclose themselves in their full asininity. With the development of radio, television, and films the disclosure is more complete —not that it makes much difference to the oafish constituencies. The most clownish performances of an Everett Dirksen, Joe McCarthy, or Barry Goldwater are taken by a wide public as exercises in sagacious statesmanship, as strokes of marvelous political acumen.

The sort of monsters I have in mind one finds on the senatorial level in Coleman Livingston ("Cole") Blease (1868-1942), of South Carolina; Huey P. Long (1893-1935), of Louisiana; James Kimble Vardaman (1861-1930), of Mississippi; Theodore G. Bilbo (1877-1947), of Mississippi; Benjamin R. Tillman (1847-1918), of South Carolina—all unbelievably uncouth, loud, noxious, ignorant, and typical of a much larger, somewhat more muted group. Professed democrats, all preached repression of the Negro. All flaunted the ordinary decencies.

If one charges that I am not playing fair by drawing examples only from the stagnant cultural swampland of the American South, then one may consider Joseph B. Foraker (1846-1917), of Ohio, a leading presidential contender incontrovertibly shown to be on the secret payroll of Standard Oil; Albert B. Fall (1861-1944), of New Mexico, on the payroll of oil buccaneers and finally miraculously jailed for accepting bribes; or Boies Penrose (1860-1921), of Pennsylvania, a saturnine political corruptionist to his fingertips—all mere samples from a much larger collection of purulent cases.

Again, if one claims that this is all in the past, that conditions are better now in the way of political personnel, we are confronted North and South—still on the senatorial level—by such smarmy creatures as Joseph R. McCarthy (1907-1957), of Wisconsin; Everett M. Dirksen (1896-), of Illinois; Thomas J. Dodd (1907-), of Connecticut, whom the Senate itself astonishingly censured for the standard practice of privately pocketing campaign contributions; wild-eyed J. Strom Thurmond (1902-), of South Carolina; Spessard L. Holland (1892-), of Florida; George A. Smathers (1913-), of Florida; Herman E. Talmadge (1913-), of Georgia; Allen J. Ellender (1890-), of Louisiana; and James O. Eastland (1904-), of Mississippi—to mention only a few of the outstanding contemporary clowns. Much if not most of the Senate, indeed, is composed of dopes, mental deviants, or rascals, as countless surveys have shown. A cool euphemism has been coined to cover the cozy situation: conflict of interest.

The House of Representatives, sometimes called "The Monkey House," is even worse, and the state legislatures in general are on the level of common slum trollops and bawds—all, however, returned to office by preponderant, often enthusiastic, popular majorities. To rake them over once again would be to flog long-dead horses. Repeated investigations have time and again disclosed the sordid facts *ad nauseam*.

American mayors became so uniformly and notoriously

bad, the local civic aroma so nauseous, that in little more than fifty years nearly half the municipalities have switched to the city manager form of government, wherein a hired professional administrator performs executive duties. James M. Curley (1874-1958), four-time mayor of Boston and once governor of Massachusetts, is pretty standard for the traditional type of American big-city mayor, with the exception that toward the end of his life he served a merited term in federal prison for mail fraud; he was prematurely released on a presidential pardon. A number of New York City mayors who sidestepped jail fled to foreign climes, one jump ahead of foot-dragging lawmen.

Queer gentry, Mafian cut-purse types, have prevailed as governors down through the years in many if not most of the states. A few of the more unbelievable of recent years have been Huey and Earl Long, of Louisiana; Mr. and Mrs. George C. Wallace of Alabama; Orval E. Faubus, of Arkansas; Claude Kirk, Jr., of Florida; and Lester G. Maddox, of Georgia. There were also Ma and Pa Ferguson, Lee "Pappy" O'Daniel, and "Alfalfa Bill" Murray. This list could be considerably extended into northern and western regions.

Two extreme personality wings may be noticed in American politics, somewhat screening the main body of politicians, seldom any better than they need to be. One large wing screens the main body by drawing invidious attention away from it and holding attention with bizarre antics, not the least of which are repeated stupendous covert raids on the rank-and-file taxpayers' dollars. The other, a very small wing, functions on such a relatively high level that it tends to validate the intrigues of their more dubious colleagues by suggesting that there is some sem-

blance of sagacity present. This latter group, today including such as J. William Fulbright and Clifford P. Case
among a score or more of others, is as much out of place in
practical politics as would be a Florence Nightingale or
Joan of Arc in a pestilent bordello, an Aristotle in a padded
cell, its sole effective function being to gain acceptance for
the light-fingered, softly shod, loose-lipped, and more or
less unhinged main body.

Have I omitted anyone? If so, it is only by failing to
catalogue all the names and to enter into details of such
shenanigans as the Bobby Baker affair, the Teapot Dome
case, the Credit Mobilier, the Military-Industrial Contract
Complex, and the like. One roaring financial scandal succeeds the other in "democratic" politics. Elsewhere they
are papered over.

Lest it be thought that what I say arises from some personal distemper, or from the theories of some doctrinal
school, it would be well, if only for the sake of company, to
set down what an authentic man of affairs had to say about
his dealings with a nationally prominent politician. This
man was the late Charles Francis Adams, of Boston, former
president of the Union Pacific Railroad, descendant of the
celebrated Adams family that contributed two national
presidents and other distinguished men. And what Adams
records in his autobiography was a fairly typical experience
of many.

"I was at once sent on to Washington to avert the
threatened action of the Government, which would have
sent the company into the hands of a receiver; and then
and there I had my first experience in the most hopeless
and repulsive work in which I ever was engaged—trans-
acting business with the United States Government, and

35

trying to accomplish something through Congressional action. My initial episode was with a prominent member of the United States Senate. This Senator is still (1912) alive, though long retired; he has a great reputation for ability, and a certain reputation, somewhat fly-blown, it is true, for rugged honesty. I can only say that I found him an ill-mannered bully, and by all odds the most covertly and dangerously corrupt man I ever had opportunity and occasion carefully to observe in public life. His grudge against the Union Pacific was that it had not retained him —he was not, as a counsel, in its pay. While he took excellent care of those competing concerns which had been wiser in this respect, he never lost an opportunity of posing as the fearless antagonist of corporations when the Union Pacific came to the front. For that man, on good and sufficient grounds, I entertained a deep dislike. He was distinctly dishonest—a senatorial bribe-taker."

(Note: It was common then, and still is, for members of Congress to be retained as lawyers of big companies, through their law firms, and to harass uncooperative companies and even industries—as in the case of Senator Dodd —with proposals for unwelcome investigations. It is, I repeat, *standard practice*.)

The faults, torts, aberrancies, and felonies of the politico, American style, are in fact so extensive as to defy cataloguing. Nobody could find the time to read about them in the necessary encyclopedic format, so large an area of space and time do they cover. What is most ludicrous about the American scenario is that it is played out under the halo of a spurious democracy, immoderately celebrated before helpless children in the public schools. These are indoctrinated with sheer balderdash. The more intelligent among

36

them subsequently become cynics. In political outlook, most intelligent people in the United States are cynics.

All this being soberly the case, unmentioned examples without number abounding, it is instructive to read what people down through history have thought about politicians. All that is different is that in the United States, as might be expected, everything assumes exaggerated proportions. If anyone should mention Hitler or Stalin as gigantic un-American examples, the reply obviously is that the United States swarms with clamorous midget Hitlers and Stalins, deterred from following in the footsteps of these Fuehrers only by the restraint of traditional institutions and the lack of a propitious moment.

So, while the United States unfortunately cannot claim a first in the matter of a Hitler, it cannot be put entirely out of the running in this respect, in view of the many noisy claimants to the role. We may be sure that if the United States ever does have a Hitler he will be bigger and better in every way—bigger gas ovens, more victims, bigger bombs. This follows from the well-established law that any American is better than any ten foreigners, any day.

We may turn, now, to what many others have said down through the centuries about the politico and his handiwork —politics. As one reads, it gradually dawns on one that here lies a large part of the explanation of why the world, in the midst of an unprecedented volume of exact knowledge, is in such a presently perilous condition. Mankind has long been going to the dogs, and one day will surely reach its destination.

I

Of Politicians

The ruler over a country of a thousand chariots must give diligent attention to business; he must be sincere; he must be economical; he must love his people; and he must provide employment for them at the proper seasons.

CONFUCIUS: Analects, I, c. 500 B.C.

Do you suppose that I should have lived as long as I have if I had moved in the sphere of public life, and conducting myself in that sphere like an honorable man, had always upheld the cause of right, and conscientiously set this end

39

above all other things? Not by a very long way, gentlemen; neither would any other man.

Socrates: Quoted in Plato's *Apology,* c. 399 B.C.

If I had engaged in politics, O men of Athens, I should have perished long ago, and done no good either to you or to myself.

Socrates: Quoted in Plato's *Apology*

. . . The proudest of politicians have the strongest desire to write speeches and bequeath compositions . . . when an orator, or a king, succeeds in acquiring the power of a Lycurgus, a Solon, or a Darius, and so winning immortality among his people as a speech writer, doesn't he deem himself a peer of the gods while still living, and do not people in later ages hold the same opinion of him when they contemplate his writings?

Plato: *Phaedrus*

That politician who curries favor with the citizens and indulges them and fawns upon them and has a presentiment of their wishes, and is skillful in gratifying them, he is esteemed as a great statesman.

Plato: *Republic,* IV

There are some politicians whom the applause of the multitude has deluded into the belief that they are really statesmen, and they are not much to be admired. . . . When a man cannot measure, and a great many others who cannot measure, declare that he is four cubits high, can he help believing them?

Ibid.

They know that no politician is honest, nor is there any champion of justice at whose side they may fight and be saved.

Ibid., VI

We shall see who are the false politicians who win popularity and pretend to be politicians and are not, and separate them from the wise king.

PLATO: *Statesman*

Men are marked out from the moment of birth to rule or be ruled.

ARISTOTLE: *Politics,* I, c. 320 B.C.

Later variants on the above by unidentified wits:
Men are marked out from the moment of birth to rule or to be ruined.

Men are marked out from the moment of birth to rule and ruin.

Goethe said: All men have the choice in life of being hammer or anvil [that is, active or passive].

A man who aspires to any high office should have three qualifications: first, he should be prepared to support the constitution of his country; second, he should have a special aptitude for the office he desires; and third, he should have virtue and justice as they are understood by his fellow-citizens.

Ibid., V

The political orator aims at establishing the expediency or the harmfulness of a proposed course of action; if he urges its acceptance, he does so on the ground that it will do good; if he urges its rejection, he does so on the ground that it will do harm; and all other points, such as whether the proposal is just or unjust, honorable or dishonorable, he brings in as subsidiary and relative to this main consideration. Parties in a law-case aim at establishing the justice or injustice of some action, and they too bring in all other points as subsidiary and relative to this one. Those who praise or attack a man aim at proving him worthy of honor or the reverse, and they too treat all other considerations with reference to this one.

ARISTOTLE: *Rhetorica,* I, 3

Political oratory is less given to unscrupulous practices than forensic, because it treats of wider issues. In a political debate the man who is forming a judgment is making a decision about his own vital interests. There is no need, therefore, to prove anything except that the facts are what the supporter of a measure maintains they are.

Ibid., II, 1

Those in power are more ambitious and manly in character than the wealthy, because they aspire to do the great deeds that their power permits them to do. Responsibility makes them more serious: they have to keep paying attention to the duties their position involves. They are dignified rather than arrogant, for the respect in which they are held inspires them with dignity and therefore with moderation —dignity being a mild and becoming form of arrogance.

If they wrong others, they wrong them not on a small but on a great scale.

Ibid., II, 17

To be able to endure odium is the first art to be learned by those who aspire to power.

SENECA: *Hercules Furens,* c. 50

They are wrong who think that politics is like an ocean voyage or a military campaign, something to be done with some particular end in view, something which leaves off as soon as that end is reached. It is not a public chore, to be got over with. It is a way of life. It is the life of a domesticated political and social creature who is born with a love for public life, with a desire for honor, with a feeling for his fellows; and it lasts as long as need be.

PLUTARCH (46-120)

Whatsoever moveth is stronger than that which is moved, and whatsoever governeth is stronger than that which is governed.

ST. ARISTIDES (fl. 2nd century):
Apology for the Christian Faith

It seems to me that to rule men is the art of arts, and the science of sciences, for man is a being diverse and manifold in character.

ST. GREGORY OF NAZIANZEN (c. 257-332):
Orations, 2, 16

It is a common experience that in the school of adversity the heart is forced to discipline itself; but when a man has achieved supreme rule, it is at once changed and puffed up by the experience of his high estate.

Pope St. Gregory I (c. 540-604):
Pastoral Care, I, x

With the rashness of ignorance the uninitiated dare to dabble in affairs of state.

John of Salisbury (c. 1115-1180):
Policraticus, I, 4, 35

There is no repose about [those in] politics, for they are ever seeking an end outside political practice, for instance power or fame. Political life neither provides our final end nor contains the happiness we seek for ourselves or others. . . . The purpose of temporal tranquillity, which well-ordered polities establish and maintain, is to give opportunities for contemplating truth.

St. Thomas Aquinas (c. 1225-1274):
Commentary on the Ethics, 10, lect. 11

A wise prince [politician] cannot, nor ought he to, keep faith when such observance may be turned against him, and when the reasons that caused him to pledge it exist no longer. If men were entirely good, this precept would not hold, but because they are bad, and will not keep faith with you, you are not bound to observe it with them.

Niccolò Machiavelli: *The Prince,* 1513

He who has known best how to employ the fox has succeeded best. But it is necessary to know well how to disguise this characteristic, and to be a great pretender and dissembler; and men are so simple, and so subject to present necessities, that he who seeks to deceive will always find some one who will allow himself to be deceived.

Ibid.

Therefore it is unnecessary for a prince [politician] to have all the good qualities I have enumerated, but it is very necessary to appear to have them. And I shall dare to say this also, that to have them and always to observe them is injurious, and that to appear to have them is useful; to appear merciful, faithful, humane, religious, upright, and to be so, but with a mind so framed that should you require not to be so, you may be able and know how to change to the opposite.

Ibid.

Everyone sees what you appear to be; few really know what you are.

Ibid.

As princes [politicians] cannot help being hated by someone, they ought, in the first place, to avoid being hated by everyone, and when they cannot compass this, they ought to endeavor with the utmost diligence to avoid the hatred of the most powerful.

Ibid.

Many consider that a wise prince [politician], when he has the opportunity, ought with craft to foster some animosity against himself, so that, having crushed it, his renown may rise higher.

Ibid.

It is necessary for a prince [politician] wishing to hold his own to know how to do wrong, and to make use of it or not according to necessity.

Ibid.

A politician . . . one that would circumvent God.
WILLIAM SHAKESPEARE: *Hamlet*, V, c. 1601

The insolence of office.
WILLIAM SHAKESPEARE: *Hamlet*, III

It is as hard and severe a thing to be a true politician as to be truly moral.
FRANCIS BACON: *The Advancement of Learning*, II, 1605

Get thee glass eyes;
And, like a scurvy politician, seem
to see the thing thou dost not.
WILLIAM SHAKESPEARE: *King Lear*, IV, 1606

A politician is the devil's quilted anvil;
He fashions all sins on him, and the blows
are never heard.
JOHN WEBSTER (c. 1580-c. 1625):
The Duchess of Malfi, III, ii, c. 1613

A Politician imitates the Devill, as the Devill imitates a cannon: wheresoever he comes to do mischiefe, he comes with his backside towardes you.
JOHN WEBSTER: *The White Devill*, III, 3, 1612

46

Men in Great Place are thrice Servants: Servants of the Sovereign or State; Servants of Fame; and Servants of Business. So as they have no Freedom; neither in their Persons, nor in their Actions, nor in their Times.

FRANCIS BACON (1561-1626): *Essays*

As there are mountebanks for the natural body, so are there mountebanks for the politic body; men that undertake great cures, and, perhaps, have been lucky in two or three experiments, but want the grounds of science, and therefore cannot hold out.

FRANCIS BACON: *Essays,* XII, 1625

I am a politician, oathes with me
Are but the tooles I worke with, I may breake
An oath by my profession.

THOMAS HAYWOOD: *The Iron Age,* II, 1632

We starve our conscience when we thrive in state.

JAMES SHIRLEY: *The Cardinal,* V, 1641

[He] was meerly a Politician, and studied only his owne ends.

SIR GEORGE BUCK: *History of the Life and Reigne of Richard III,* I, 17, 1646

Fate often makes up for the eminence of office by the inferiority of the officeholder.

BALTASAR GRACIAN:
The Art of Worldly Wisdom, CLXXXII, 1647

47

The lust of government is the greatest lust.

JAMES HARRINGTON:
The Commonwealth of Oceana, 1656

In friendship false, implacable in hate,
Resolved to ruin or to rule the state.

JOHN DRYDEN: *Absalom and Achitophel*, I, 1682

For politicians neither love nor hate.

Ibid.

There are hardly two Creatures of a more differing Species than the same Man, when he is pretending to a Place, and when he is in possession of it.

LORD HALIFAX (1633-1695): *Works* (1912)

Some Places have such a corrupting Influence upon the Man, that it is a supernatural thing to resist it.

LORD HALIFAX: *Ibid.*

The mob are statesmen, and their statesmen sots.

DANIEL DEFOE: *The True-Born Englishman*, II, 1701

Rulers are men before God and gods before men.

NATHANIEL AMES: *Almanac*, 1704

Arbitrary power is the natural object of temptation to a prince [politician], as wine or women to a young fellow, or a bribe to a judge, or avarice to old age, or vanity to a woman.

JONATHAN SWIFT: *Thoughts on Various Subjects*, 1706

48

Is there not some chosen curse,
Some hidden thunder in the stores of Heaven,
Red with uncommon wrath, to blast the man,
Who owes his greatness to his country's ruin?
JOSEPH ADDISON: *Cato,* I, 1713

When vice prevails and impious men bear sway,
The post of honor is a private station.
Ibid., IV

Every time I fill a vacant office I make a hundred malcontents and one ingrate.
LOUIS XIV OF FRANCE (1638-1715), quoted c. 1752
in Voltaire's *Century of Louis XIV*

He gave it for his opinion, "that whoever could make two ears of corn, or two blades of grass, to grow upon a spot of ground where only one grew before, would deserve better of mankind, and do more essential service to his country, than the whole race of politicians put together."
JONATHAN SWIFT: *Gulliver's Travels,* II, 1726

They politics like ours profess,
The greater prey upon the less.
MATTHEW GREEN (1696-1737): *The Grotto,* 1732

Jack in office is a great man.
THOMAS FULLER (1608-1661): *Gnomologia*

They that buy an office must sell something.
Ibid.

That politician tops his part,
Who readily can lie with art;
The man's proficient in his trade;
His pow'r is strong, his fortune's made.

JOHN GAY: *Fables,* II, 1738

Nothing appears more surprising to those who consider human affairs with a philosophical eye than the easiness with which the many are governed by the few.

DAVID HUME: *Essays Moral and Political,* I, 1741

Old politicians chew on wisdom past.

ALEXANDER POPE (1688-1744)

To govern mankind one must not overrate them; and to please an audience as a speaker, one must not over-value it. When I first came into the House of Commons, I respected that assembly as a venerable one, and felt a certain awe upon me; but upon better acquaintance that awe soon vanished, and I discovered that of the five hundred and sixty, not above thirty could understand reason; . . . that those thirty only required plain common sense, dressed up in good language; and that all the others only required flowing and harmonious periods, whether they conveyed any meaning or not; having ears to hear, but not sense enough to judge.

LORD CHESTERFIELD (1694-1773): *Letters,* 1748

Politicians neither love nor hate. Interest, not sentiment, directs them.

Ibid.

The greatest art of a politician is to render vices service-
able to virtue.

LORD BOLINGBROKE (1678-1751)

Ignorance leads Men into a Party, and Shame keeps
them from getting out again.

BENJAMIN FRANKLIN: *Poor Richard's Almanack,* 1753

Among politicians the esteem of religion is profitable;
the principles of it are troublesome.

BENJAMIN WHICHCOTE:
Moral and Religious Aphorisms, 1753

Ask of politicians the ends for which laws were originally
designed, and they will answer that the laws were designed
as a protection for the poor and the weak, against the oppression of the rich and powerful. But surely no pretense
can be so ridiculous; a man might as well tell me he has
taken off my load, because he has changed the burden.

EDMUND BURKE:
A Vindication of Natural Society, 1756

The first mistake in public business is the going into it.

BENJAMIN FRANKLIN: *Poor Richard's Almanack,* 1758

I do not admire politicians; but when they are excellent
in their way, one cannot help allowing them their due.

HORACE WALPOLE: Letter to the Earl of Hertford, 1763

Every public man pays tribute to malignity, but he is
rewarded in honors and gold.

VOLTAIRE: *Philosophical Dictionary,* 1764

Survey the Patriot, with indignant Soul
Who bids the thunders of his Censures roll
Full o'er the Statesman's Head—laments the Realm,
Where Pride and Folly blunder at the Helm;
Eyes with disdain the ministerial Race,
By Vice and Meanness climbing into Place;
And paints in Elegy's enthusiast Strains
Destruction hov'ring o'er his native Plains.

> EDWARD BURNABY GREENE: *The Politician,* 1766

. . . Scorpions of the State

> *Ibid.*

The violation of party faith, is, of itself, too common to excite surprise or indignation.

> JUNIUS: *Letters,* c. 1768-1772

Political friendships are so well understood that we can hardly pity the simplicity they deceived.

> *Ibid.*

The deepest politician toils but for a momentary rattle.

> HORACE WALPOLE: Letter to Horace Mann, 1777

What a dreadful thing it is for such a wicked little imp as man to have absolute power!

> HORACE WALPOLE: Letter to William Mason, 1778

. . . that insidious and crafty animal, vulgarly called a statesman or politician, whose councils are directed by the momentary fluctuations of affairs.

> ADAM SMITH (1723-1790)

The vigour of the ministry is like the vigour of a grave-digger—the tomb becomes more ready and more wide for every effort which they make.

SYDNEY SMITH: *Peter Plymley's Letters,* 1807

Meetings consisting of some half a dozen scurvy pot-house politicians.

WASHINGTON IRVING:
Knickerbocker's History of New York, IV, 6, 1809

A cool blooded and crafty politician, when he would be thoroughly revenged on his enemy, makes the injuries which have been inflicted, not on himself, but on others, the pretext of his attack.

C. C. COLTON: *The Lacon,* 1820

An upright [government] minister asks, *what* recommends a man: a corrupt minister, *who.*

Ibid.

Whenever a man has cast a longing eye on offices, a rottenness begins in his conduct.

THOMAS JEFFERSON: Letter to Tench Coxe, 1820

In politics, an absurdity is not an impediment.

NAPOLEON BONAPARTE (1769-1821)

The great difficulty with politics is that there are no established principles.

NAPOLEON BONAPARTE

So long as the present system of electioneering continues the Legislature must be made up of all kinds of materials.

Massachusetts Spy, January 18, 1826

Few politicians die, and none resign.

THOMAS JEFFERSON (1743-1826)

Political distinction is like the pyramids where none can hope to reach the top but eagles or reptiles.

Unnamed author quoted by RALPH WALDO EMERSON:
Journals, 1827

A politician, where factions run high, is interested not for the whole people, but for his own section of it. The rest are, in his view, strangers, enemies, or rather pirates.

T. B. MACAULAY: *Hallam,* 1828

A new race of men is springing up to govern the nation; they are the hunters after popularity, men ambitious, not of the honor so much as of the profits of office—the demagogues, whose principles hang laxly upon them, and who follow not so much what is right as what leads to temporary vulgar applause.

JOSEPH STORY: *Commentaries on the Constitution of the United States,* 1833

That a man before whom the two paths of literature and politics lie open, and who might hope for eminence in either, should choose politics, and quit literature, seems to me madness.

T. B. MACAULAY: Letter to T. F. Ellis, 1835

The very existence of government at all infers inequality. The citizen who is preferred to office becomes the superior of those who are not, so long as he is the repository of power.

JAMES FENIMORE COOPER:
The American Democrat, VII, 1838

Contact with the affairs of state is one of the most corrupting of the influences to which men are exposed.

Ibid., VIII

The demagogue is usually sly, a detractor of others, a professor of humility and disinterestedness, a great stickler for equality as respects all above him, a man who acts in corners, and avoids open and manly expositions of his course, calls blackguards gentlemen, and gentlemen folks, appeals to passions and prejudices rather than reason, and is in all respects a man of intrigue and deception, of sly cunning and management.

Ibid., XXI, 1838

An important art of politicians is to find new names for institutions which under old names have become odious to the public.

CHARLES MAURICE DE TALLEYRAND-PERIGORD
(1754-1838)

A politician must often talk and act before he has thought and read. He may be very ill-informed respecting a question; all his notions about it may be vague and inaccurate; but speak he must; and if he is a man of talents, of

tact, and of intrepidity, he soon finds that, even under such circumstances, it is possible to speak successfully.
T. B. MACAULAY: *Gladstone on Church and State,* 1839

. . . A Whig Editor, a bar-room wrangler, a stump orator, a noisy, brawling pot-house politician. . . .
Representative SAMUEL GORDON, New York:
Congressional Globe, p. 264, App., August 25, 1841

Timid and interested politicians think much more about the security of their seats than about the security of their country.
T. B. MACAULAY:
Speech in the House of Commons, 1842

To place and power all public spirit tends,
In place and power all public spirit ends;
Like hardy plants, that love the air and sky,
When out, 'twill thrive—but taken *in,* 'twill die!
THOMAS MOORE (1779-1852) : *Corruption*

A statesman makes the occasion, but the occasion makes the politician.
GEORGE S. HILLIARD: *Eulogy on Daniel Webster,* 1852

Concealment, evasion, factious combinations, the surrender of convictions to party objects, and the systematic pursuit of expediency are things of daily occurrence among men of the highest character, once embarked in the contentions of political life.
ROBERT LOWE: Editorial, *London Times,*
February 7, 1852

No man is good enough to govern another man without
that other's consent.
ABRAHAM LINCOLN: Speech, Peoria, 1854

Are those really congressmen? are those the great
    judges? is that the President?
Then I will sleep awhile yet—for I see that
    These States sleep.
WALT WHITMAN: *To the States,* 1860

. . . a host of loud-mouthed, pot-house politicians.
SAMUEL MORDECAI: *Virginia in By-gone Days,* 1860

This struggle and scramble for office, for a way to live
without work, will finally test the strength of our institutions.
ABRAHAM LINCOLN: To W. H. Herndon, 1861

Not pot-house politicians only but profound thinkers,
declared the Government permanently crippled.
Representative SAMUEL SHELLABARGER, Ohio:
Congressional Globe, p. 690/1, February 6, 1862

Politicians are like the bones of a horse's fore-shoulder
—not a straight one in it.
WENDELL PHILLIPS: Speech, 1864

Party spirit enlists a man's virtues in the cause of his
vices.
RICHARD WHATELY (1787-1863)

Politicians are a set of men who have interests aside from

57

the interests of the people and who, to say the most of them, are, taken as a mass, at least one step removed from honest men.

ABRAHAM LINCOLN (1809-1865)

The farmer imagines power and place are fine things. But the President has paid dear for his White House. It has commonly cost him all his peace, and the best of his manly attributes. To preserve for a short time so conspicuous an appearance before the world, he is content to eat dust before the real masters who stand behind the throne.

RALPH WALDO EMERSON: *Compensation,* 1865

I'm not a politician and my other habits are good.

ARTEMUS WARD (1834-1867) : *Fourth of July Oration*

The more I see of the representatives of the people, the more I admire my dogs.

ALPHONSE DE LAMARTINE (1790-1869)

The world is weary of statesmen whom democracy has degraded into politicians.

BENJAMIN DISRAELI: *Lothair,* XVII, 1870

A pot-house politician should represent us at the court of St. James.

JOAQUIN MILLER: *Life Amongst the Modocs,* 1873

It is the misfortune of all miscellaneous political combinations, that with the purest motives of their more generous members are ever mixed the most sordid interests and the fiercest passions of mean confederates.

EDWARD GEORGE EARLE BULWER-LYTTON (1803-1873)

I delight in the barbaric simplicity of our native legislators. . . . I always feel a certain vague sense of personal
fear when in close proximity to one of our south-western
congressmen, as I do when I meet a Sioux warrior on the
plains. . . . I feel it nowhere in Europe, and only among
the Bedouins in Africa. Hence, how much more amusing
our politicians are than yours.

HENRY ADAMS: Letter to Charles Milnes Gaskell,
February 13, 1874

Great politicians owe their reputation, if not to pure
chance, then to circumstances at least which they themselves could not foresee.

OTTO VON BISMARCK: To M. de Blowitz
of *The London Times,* c. 1875

As long as I count the votes what are you going to do
about it? Say.

WILLIAM MARCY TWEED (1823-1878), Tammany boss

You can't get anything without paying for it.

WILLIAM MARCY TWEED, then New York State Senator

To scholars who become politicians the comic role is
usually assigned; they have to be the good conscience of a
state policy.

FRIEDRICH W. NIETZSCHE:
Human-All-too-Human, I, 1878

We cannot safely leave politics to politicians, or political
economy to college professors.

HENRY GEORGE: *Progress and Poverty,* 1879

The word "politician" is used in a bad sense in America as applied to people who . . . are skilled in the art of "wire-pulling."

SIR GEORGE CAMPBELL: *White and Black,* 1879

The members who composed it [any Democratic Party National Convention prior to the Civil War] were, seven-eighths of them, the meanest kind of bawling and blowing officeholders, office-seekers, pimps, malignants, conspirators, murderers, fancy-men, custom-house clerks, contractors, kept-editors, spaniels well-train'd to carry and fetch, jobbers, infidels, disunionists, terrorists, mail-riflers, slave-catchers, pushers of slavery, creatures of the President, creatures of would-be Presidents, spies, bribers, compromisers, lobbyers, sponges, ruin'd sports, expell'd gamblers, policy-backers, monte-dealers, duellists, carriers of conceal'd weapons, deaf men, pimpled men, scarr'd inside with vile disease, gaudy outside with gold chains made from the people's money and harlots' money twisted together; crawling, serpentine men, the lousy combinings and born freedom-sellers of the earth.

WALT WHITMAN: *Origins of Attempted Secession,*
c. 1880

The danger is not that a particular class is unfit to govern. Every class is unfit to govern.

LORD ACTON: Letter to Mary Gladstone, 1881

I suppose every man who has looked on at the game has been struck by the remarkable way in which politics deteriorate the moral tone of everyone who mixes in them. The deterioration is far more marked than in any other occupation I know except the turf, stock-jobbing, and gambling. I imagine the reason in each case to be the same. It is the curse of politics that what one man gains, another man loses. On such conditions you can create not even an average morality. Politicians as a class must be as mean as card-sharpers, turf-men, or Wall Street curbstone operators. There is no respectable industry in existence which will not average a high morality. . . . I have never known a young man go into politics who was not the worse for it. . . . They all try to be honest, and then are tripped up by the dishonest; or they try to be dishonest (i.e., practical politicians) and degrade their own natures. In the first case they become disappointed and bitter; in the other they lose self-respect. My conclusion is that no man should be in politics unless he would honestly rather not be there. Public service should be a *corvée*; a disagreeable necessity. The satisfaction should consist in getting out of it.

HENRY ADAMS: Letter to Henry Cabot Lodge, November 15, 1881

Public officers are the servants and agents of the people, to execute the laws which the people have made.

GROVER CLEVELAND: Acceptance speech for nomination as Governor of New York, 1882

When I want to buy up any politicians I always find the anti-monopolists the most purchasable. They don't come so high.

WILLIAM H. VANDERBILT: To two newspaper reporters aboard his special train approaching Chicago, as reported in the *Chicago Daily News*, October 9, 1882

61

Politics is perhaps the only profession for which no preparation is thought necessary.

ROBERT LOUIS STEVENSON (1850-1894):
Familiar Studies of Men and Books, 1882

Two kinds of men generally best succeed in political life; men of no principle, but of great talent; and men of no talent, but of one principle—that of obedience to their superiors.

WENDELL PHILLIPS (1811-1884)

A politician weakly and amiably in the right, is no match for a politician tenaciously and pugnaciously in the wrong.

EDWIN PERCY WHIPPLE (1819-1886)

A politician looks for the success of his party; a statesman for that of his country.

JAMES FREEMAN CLARKE (1810-1888)

The difference between a politician and a statesman is: a politician thinks of the next election and a statesman thinks of the next generation.

JAMES FREEMAN CLARKE

The statesman wishes to steer, while the politician is satisfied to drift.

JAMES FREEMAN CLARKE

An honest politician is one who, when he is bought, will stay bought.

SIMON CAMERON (1799-1889), Republican boss of Pennsylvania and United States Senator

He thinks like a Tory and talks like a Radical, and that's so important nowadays.

OSCAR WILDE: *Lady Windermere's Fan,* II, 1893

In order to obtain and hold power a man must love it. Thus the effort to get it is not likely to be coupled with goodness, but with the opposite qualities of pride, craft and cruelty. Without hypocrisy, lying, punishments, prisons, fortresses and murders, no new power can arise and no existing one hold its own.

LEO N. TOLSTOY:
The Kingdom of God Is Within You, 1893

Government is an association of men who do violence to the rest of us.

Ibid.

The [political] boss has the courage of the brute, or he would not be boss; but when it comes to a moral issue he is the biggest coward in the lot. The bigger the brute the more abject its terror at what it does not understand.

JACOB A. RIIS (1849-1914):
The Making of an American, 1901

Many who think they are workers in politics are really merely tools.

LORD SALISBURY (1830-1903)

To be a chemist you must study chemistry; to be a lawyer or a physician you must study law or medicine; but to be a politician you need only to study your own interests.

MAX O'RELL (pseudonym of Paul Blouet)
(1848-1903)

Politician. An eel in the fundamental mud upon which the superstructure of organized society is reared. . . . As compared with the statesman, he suffers the disadvantage of being alive.

AMBROSE BIERCE: *The Devil's Dictionary,* 1906

There is always some basic principle that will ultimately get the Republican party together. If my observations are worth anything, that basic principle is the cohesive power of public plunder.

A. J. McLAURIN: Speech, United States Senate, May, 1906

It is inexcusable for scientists to torture animals; let them make their experiments on journalists and politicians.

HENRIK IBSEN (1828-1906)

And yet, what has the Senate done—the Senate, with its high-flown pretenses of reverence for the Constitution? It has so legislated and so refrained from legislating that more than half of all the wealth created by the American people belongs to less than 1 per cent of them; that the income of the average American family has sunk to less than six hundred dollars a year; that of our more than twenty-seven million children of school age, less than twelve millions go to school, and more than two millions work in mines, shops and factories.

DAVID GRAHAM PHILLIPS: *The Treason of the Senate,* 1906

The greatest single hold of "the interests" is the fact that they are the "campaign contributors"—the men who supply the money for "keeping the party together," and for "getting out the vote." Did you ever think where the millions for watchers, spellbinders, halls, processions, posters, pamphlets, that are spent in national, state and local campaigns come from? Who pays the big election expenses of your congressman, of the men you send to the legislature to elect senators? Do you imagine those who foot those huge bills are fools? Don't you know that they make sure of getting their money back, with interest, compound upon compound? . . . The bulk of the money for the "political trust" comes from "the interests." "The interests" will give only to the "political trust."

Ibid.

A scurvy lot they are [in the United States Senate], are they not, with their smirking and cringing and voluble palaver about God and patriotism and their eager offerings of endowments for hospitals and colleges whenever the American people so much as looks hard in their direction!

Ibid.

He knows nothing; and he thinks he knows everything. That points clearly to a political career.
GEORGE BERNARD SHAW: *Major Barbara,* 1907

Fleas can be taught nearly anything that a Congressman can.
MARK TWAIN (1835-1910)

It could probably be shown by facts and figures that there is no distinctly native criminal class except Congress.
MARK TWAIN

Reader, suppose you were an idiot; and suppose you were a member of Congress; but I repeat myself.

MARK TWAIN

A dead politician is the noblest work of God.

Author unidentified, c. 1910

The masters of the government of the United States are the combined capitalists and manufacturers of the United States. It is written over every intimate page of the records of Congress, it is written all through the history of conferences at the White House, that the suggestions of economic policy in this country have come from one source, not many sources. The benevolent guardians, the kind-hearted trustees who have taken the troubles of government off our hands, have become so conspicuous that almost anybody can write out a list of them. They have become so conspicuous that their names are mentioned upon almost every political platform. The men who have undertaken the interesting job of taking care of us do not force us to requite them with anonymously direct gratitude. We know them by name.

WOODROW WILSON: Speech, 1912, published 1913
in *The New Freedom*, III

The most successful politician is he who says what everybody is thinking most often and in the loudest voice.

THEODORE ROOSEVELT (1858-1919)

The truth is that a very large proportion of candidates for all offices everywhere are in a perpetual state of fear. Most of them are frightened for fear that, inadvertently,

66

they will make some "break" that will put them out of
politics. And, of course, most of them stay scared that way
after they are elected, because there is always the necessity
of being renominated and reelected.

FRANK R. KENT: *The Great Game of Politics,* 1923

Senators and Congressmen fear to offend large and powerful interests or groups in their states, and their votes are
largely moulded by their fear. They may have had financial assistance in their campaigns from these groups, and
feel under obligations to help them, or they may want
financial assistance in their next fight and fear to offend
groups that may damage them politically either by con-
tributing money to the other side or by swinging votes
against them.

Ibid.

. . . from the time a candidate conceives the idea of becoming a candidate until the day he is forced out of politics
there is no chance for him to be wholly honest, frank, and
natural with voters. From the start he humbugs them. . . .

Ibid.

. . . it is not the fault of the candidates. Many of them are
honest, courageous, and sincere, with a real desire for public service. The chief trouble is the utter impossibility of
appealing squarely to the intelligence of the voters and
getting an impartial verdict on merit. It simply cannot be
done. The voters are not like that. Notoriously, most of
them vote from prejudice. . . .

Ibid.

The Washington correspondents—I can say this without embarrassment because I am not one of them—are as a body pretty high-grade men. It is certainly not exaggeration to say that in character, in breeding, and brains they are superior, individually and collectively, to the United States Senate. Most of them are more worth while and interesting to talk to than most Senators. Nor is it extravagant to say that it would be possible to pick a better Cabinet out of the press gallery than has been in Washington in this generation at least, though when you come to think them over that is not a very high tribute.

FRANK R. KENT: *Political Behavior,* 1928

The mere fact that the name and the face of a candidate are familiar to the voters is in itself worth votes, regardless of what he has done, who he is, what he stands for, what is behind him, or who may be running against him. . . . there is a not inconsiderable number of voters who in every election vote for the man whose picture they have become accustomed to and whose name is well known to them—and for no other reasons. . . . They have a minimum not only of political intelligence but of any sort of intelligence.

Ibid.

. . . while there is in politics ample room for men of brains and character, and while the richest rewards of the political game are not beyond their reach, these qualities are by no means essential to success; that very often the men who most conspicuously lack both brains and character have risen to the apex over men who had both; that given certain political advantages the shallowest and most ignoble can easily triumph over the most brilliant and high minded; that unless the recognized political rules are observed, and the general laws of politics obeyed, the more character and capacity a candidate for office possesses the greater his handicap.

Ibid.

The politician is an acrobat. He keeps his balance by saying the opposite of what he does.

MAURICE BARRÈS (1862-1923) : *Mes Cahiers,* XII

Those who are in Albany [capital of New York State] escaped Sing Sing [prison], and those who are in Sing Sing were on their way to Albany.

ELBERT HUBBARD:
Roycroft Dictionary and Book of Epigrams, 1923

A politician who steals is worse than a thief. He is a fool. With the grand opportunities all around for a man with political pull, there's no excuse for stealin' a cent.

GEORGE WASHINGTON PLUNKITT (1842-1924),
quondam chief of Tammany Hall

It was the essence of the courtier's art and mystery that he flattered his employer in order to victimize him, yielded to him in order to rule him. The politician under democracy does precisely the same thing. His business is never what it pretends to be. Ostensibly he is an altruist devoted whole-heartedly to the service of his fellow-men, and so abjectly public-spirited that his private interest is nothing to him. Actually he is a sturdy rogue whose principal, and often sole aim in life is to butter his parsnips.

H. L. MENCKEN: *Notes on Democracy,* 1926

Contemplating such a body as the national House of Representatives one sees only a group of men who have compromised with honour—in brief, a group of male Magdalens. They have been broken to the goose-step. They have learned how to leap through the hoops of professional job-mongers and Prohibitionist blackmailers. They have kept silent about good causes, and spoken in causes they knew to be evil. The higher they rise, the further they fall. The occasional mavericks, thrown in by miracle, last a session, and then disappear. The old Congressman, the veteran of genuine influence and power, is either one who is so stupid that the ideas of the mob are his own ideas, or one so far gone in charlatanry that he is unconscious of his shame.

Ibid.

Politics makes strange bedfellows rich.
WAYNE G. HAISLEY: *New Teeth in Old Saws,* c. 1928

Now and then an innocent man is sent to the legislature.
FRANK McKINNEY ("KIN") HUBBARD (1868-1930)

The election isn't very far off when a candidate can recognize you across the street.
FRANK McKINNEY ("KIN") HUBBARD

From a politician's Primer
        New thoughts excite
        The voters' dread.
        Be sure you're trite,
        And go ahead.
AXIPHILES: *New York World,* October 7, 1930

70

In politics we must choose between the strong man whose real interests are elsewhere and who will leave office the moment bigger opportunity beckons, and the weakling who will cling because he can't hold a job anywhere else. Public office is the last refuge of the incompetent.

BOIES PENROSE, United States Senator and Pennsylvania political boss: Quoted in *Collier's Weekly*, February 14, 1931

A politician is like quicksilver; if you try to put your finger on him, you will find nothing under it.

AUSTIN O'MALLEY (1858-1932)

The American government is a rule of the people, by the people, for the boss.

AUSTIN O'MALLEY

The statesman shears the sheep, the politician skins them.

AUSTIN O'MALLEY

In politics it is difficult sometimes to decide whether the politicians are humorless hypocrites or hypocritical humorists; whether in fooling the people they also fool themselves, which means that both the politicians and the people are stupid, or whether the politicians are smarter than the people and know exactly what they are doing. Probably the truth is the politicians are smarter, but not much smarter, and that both are without any humor whatever.

FRANK R. KENT: *Baltimore Sun,* July 24, 1932

You cannot adopt Politics as a profession and remain honest.

LOUIS MCHENRY HOWE, American Presidential
Secretary: Speech, January 17, 1933

A politician will do anything to keep his job—even become a patriot.

WILLIAM RANDOLPH HEARST:
Editorial, August 28, 1933

During Walpole's lifetime the most common charge against him was that he degraded British politics by an unparalleled corruption, and this accusation has gone on echoing ever since. How little justice there was in singling him out for special condemnation has been shown by several modern writers. Of course it cannot be disputed that he bought votes in Parliament and at elections; but he bribed no more lavishly than his immediate predecessors and successors, and much less lavishly, though much more shrewdly, than did George the Third during the first twenty years of his reign.

FREDERICK SCOTT OLIVER: *Politics and Politicians,* 1934

A politician, like a clergyman, is wise not to jest too freely about the mysteries of his vocation. The piety of a ribald priest and the honesty of a cynic statesman are always suspect, though occasionally the ribaldry of the one and the cynicism of the other are no more than thin veneers.

Ibid.

The politician in the practice of his peculiar art must take account of several outside forces; and among these is morals, which can never be kept out of any discussion on human affairs.

Ibid.

Few men are placed in such fortunate circumstances as to be able to gain office, or to keep it for any length of time, without misleading or bamboozling the people.

Ibid.

The British blend of representative with party government leaves a politician no choice but to use his best endeavours to ruin his opponent. This is the plain truth. . . .

Ibid.

The prime motive of the politician is not to do good to humanity or even to his own country, but simply to gain power for himself. Yet he will inevitably fail if he refuses homage to the moral standards of his particular age.

Ibid.

In taking stock of a politician the first question is not whether he was a good man who used righteous means, but whether he was successful in gaining power, in keeping it, and in governing; whether, in short, he was skilful at his particular craft or a bungler.

Ibid.

The century of Louis the Eleventh, of Commines, of the Borgias, the Medici, Pope Julius the Second and Machiavelli shows a scene that in many of its aspects appears extremely different from our own. But the predominant aim of politicians then, as now, was to rid themselves of their opponents, to gain power and to keep it. Though our politicians use less lethal methods, their objects are still the same. Killing was then one of the recognized ways of getting rid of a dangerous rival, just as attacks on his public and private honour are to-day. But there was probably no more malice and hatred among the rivals than there is now. Caesar Borgia murdered his treacherous confederates, just as Giovanpagolo murdered his nephews and kinsmen, just as Lenin murdered the Imperial Family and the middle-classes, not from hatred or revenge, but simply because he found them in his way.

Ibid.

Men who are engaged in public life must necessarily aim at reducing opposition to a minimum, and one of the most obvious means to that end is by misrepresenting, discrediting or ruining their opponents.

Ibid.

The hatreds of political opponents, like their occasional ebullitions of bonhommie, are shallow-rooted plants.

Ibid.

Politicians are like the pedants in Montaigne's essay: no one has a good word to say for them.

Ibid.

The notion that politics is all a cheat and that politicians are no better than welshers has subsisted ever since the beginning.

Ibid.

A politician may disregard the random, incoherent censures of the common herd; but it is a different matter when high-brows prove their case against him with a wealth of instances and a withering scorn. According to these critics he lacks natural intelligence as well as education; he has no foresight, no constancy of purpose beyond the pursuit of his own advantage; he is not only ignorant of first principles, but indifferent to every kind of principle; he picks up the first expedient his eye lights on, and when it fails him, picks up another a few days later which is in direct antagonism to the first.

Ibid.

It is true that the politician, in his professional character, does not always, or even very often, conform to the most approved pattern of private conduct.

Ibid.

The politician is never his own master, as men are who seek their fortune in private adventures. The most complete victory does not make him the possessor, but only the custodian, of that strange monster which he calls his country.

Ibid.

. . . a positive and strict veracity is impossible for the politician; for truthfulness even forbids you to allow the person you are dealing with to deceive himself.

Ibid.

But their [i.e., Russian communist politicians] main purpose was ambition, and under this impulse they have acted

75

according to the rules:—fooling and blinding the people; modifying and reversing their policies in order to retain popularity; quarrelling among themselves for pre-eminence; getting rid of their rivals without scruple when opportunity offered; behaving in short as politicians have always behaved since political society was first instituted.

Ibid.

Lenin . . . used fraud and violence because no other methods were available.

Ibid.

No politician has ever yet been able to rule his country, nor has any country ever yet been able to face the world, upon the principles of the Sermon on the Mount.

Ibid.

Every politician learns before he is out of his nonage that it is impossible to cut sheer across a nation's history and start afresh from a clean edge.

Ibid.

Men who are engaged in public life must necessarily aim at reducing opposition to a minimum, and one of the most obvious means to that end is by misrepresenting, discrediting or ruining their opponents.

Ibid.

The danger lies in ignoring the Old Adam that survives in every nation under the sun; in slurring over the guilt of prophets and pedagogues, of journalists hunting for sensations, and soldiers whom a professional fanaticism had driven out of their wits. As a consequence of this there has been a tendency to heap far more than a fair share of the discredit for what has lately happened upon politicians and the methods their art employed.

Ibid.

I never lack material for my humor column when Congress is in session.

WILL ROGERS (1879-1935)

One of the evils of democracy is that you have to endure the man you elected whether you like him or not.

WILL ROGERS

The aim of a politician is the same as that of almost all other men. It is his own advancement and advantage. Just as the prince in Machiavelli's day sought benefits for himself as practically his only goal, so, in America to-day, the politician seeks his own advantage almost entirely. . . . It is well for the politician consistently to bear in mind that advantage to himself is his only goal. He should consider all proposals, all projects, all suggested measures, on that basis.

J. H. WALLIS: *The Politician*, I, 1935

How should a politician look upon these deaths that occur on primary or election days as machine-guns sweep the streets or pistols bark at or near the polling places? Generally speaking, an American, unless he is murdered himself, does not take murders seriously. But the wise and instructed politician does take these murders seriously. Frequently he issues statements about them, and, if the dead are his partisans, he attends the funerals with scrupulous solemnity. For such funerals he dresses himself with great care and usually manages to have a newspaper photographer catch him as he leaves the church or house at which the services have been held.

Ibid.

Convictions in a politician are an infirmity and may prove a very serious injury.

Ibid., IV

The skillful politician cannot be called either sincere or insincere. Sincerity does not enter into his situation at all.

Ibid.

The wise and clever politician makes the passions and prejudices of his constituents one of his principal assets. Nearly all people vote not according to the best interests of the community or even according to their own best interests as decided by calm and logical reasoning, but according to their passions and prejudices.

Ibid., VI

Race prejudice, class prejudice, religious prejudice, are three great forces to which the politician may appeal successfully.

Ibid.

The wise and intelligent politician sees that he is thoroughly informed concerning the religious complexion of his constituency and acts accordingly.

Ibid.

One class that comes in for powerful attack year after year is that of plotters, the conspirators, who are scheming and working ceaselessly against the program and the progress of the virtuous politician.

Ibid., VII

The sagacious politician knows the universal appeal of the children. He must display, he does display, a tenderness for children. One frequently reads of politicians' kissing the babies of the voters of their districts. As a matter of fact, few babies are so kissed, but they are admired and shown delicate attentions. The politician continually thinks of ways in which he may be kind to children—not secret ways.

Ibid., X

The politician chooses his Menace as he does his party, his principles, his food, his clothing, his manner of living. That is, he chooses a Menace that will be approved by his constituents.

Ibid., XII

As our politicians are of infinite variety, differing in party affiliation and in many other respects, and as all the skillful ones (in the North) claim that they resemble Lincoln or have Lincoln's support for their views, we find that Lincoln is on a good many sides at once.

Ibid., XIII

A politician ought to be able to salute Catholics, all sects of Protestants, Jews—as he could salute Mohammedans, Buddhists, Taoists, Shintoists, and all other religious ists,

79

if they were numerous enough to count at the ballot box. But the greetings must be sweetly general in nature. One can't very well be specifically for and against transubstantiation at the same time.

Ibid., XV

The Political Boss

You sell 'em out; you turn over the whole thing—the city, its property, and its people—to Business, to the big fellows; to the business leaders of the people. You deliver not only franchises, privileges, private rights and public property, and values, Boss: you—all of you together—have delivered the government itself to these men, so that today this city, this State, and the national government represent, normally, not the people, not the great mass of common folk, who need protection, but—Business; preferably bad business, privileged business; a class, a privileged class.

LINCOLN STEFFENS (1866-1936)

That's the system. It's an organization of social treason, and the political boss is the chief traitor. . . . They can't buy the people—too many of them; so they buy the people's leaders, and the disloyalty of the political boss is the key to the whole thing.

LINCOLN STEFFENS

There is but one way for a newspaper man to look at a politician, and that is down.

FRANK H. SIMONDS (1878-1936),

Politicians have no politics.

G. K. CHESTERTON: *Autobiography,* 1936

Politicians. Little Tin Gods on Wheels.
RUDYARD KIPLING (1865-1936) : *Public Waste*

As it was in the beginning,
Is today official sinning,
And shall be for evermore.
RUDYARD KIPLING: *A General Summary*

That the politicians are permitted to carry on the same old type of disgraceful campaign from year to year is as insulting to the people as would be a gang of thieves coming back to a town they had robbed, staging a parade, and inviting citizens to fall in and cheer.
EDGAR WATSON HOWE (1853-1937)

The cynical politicians of Europe view not only us, but all other non-European nations, as unsophisticated yokels.
JOHN FRANCIS NEYLAN:
The Politician, Enemy of Mankind, 1938

If there is one thing that terrifies a politician, it is the thought of losing his easy and luxurious berth, being taken out of the limelight and relegated to the obscurity from which he came. The prospect of having to earn whatever money he gets and pay taxes like other people brings on a cold chill and makes him almost human.
Ibid.

Additionally, we find that not only are there no godlike men, but that the direction of the destinies of the nation has been placed in the hands, almost without exception, of men who not only accomplished nothing in their private lives but who, in most instances, were utter failures.
Ibid.

The politicians were talking themselves red, white and blue in the face.

CLARE BOOTHE LUCE (1903-   )

Sooner or later all politicians die of swallowing their own lies.

CLARE BOOTHE LUCE: *Europe in the Spring,* 1940

One of the principal qualifications for a political job is that the applicant know nothing much about what he is expected to do.

TERRY M. TOWNSEND:
The Doctor Looks at the Citizen, 1940

All you will get from a group of [political] ministers is the greatest common platitude.

THOMAS JONES: Oxford conference, 1941

If you intend to be a grafter, I trust that your scientific training will prompt you to be a good one—and not one of those catch-as-catch-can thieves who gets caught in his first dereliction and thereby brings disgrace on his Alma Mater and discomfort to himself and his family.

LENT D. UPSON: *How to Graft: A Letter from a Dean of Public Administration to His Graduates,* 1942

After damning politicians up hill and down dale for forty years, as rogues and vagabonds, frauds and scoundrels, I sometimes suspect that, like everyone else, I often expect too much of them. Though faith and confidence are surely more or less foreign to my nature, I not infrequently find myself looking to them to be able, diligent, candid, and even honest. Plainly enough, that is too large an order, as anyone must realize who reflects upon the manner in which they reach public office.

H. L. MENCKEN: *Generally Political,* 1944

They are chosen normally for quite different reasons, the chief of which is simply their power to impress and enchant the intellectually underprivileged.

Ibid.

Those problems [of statecraft] demand for their solution —when they are soluble at all, which is not often—a high degree of technical proficiency, and with it there should go an adamantine kind of integrity, for the temptations of a public official are almost as cruel as those of a glamour girl or a dipsomaniac. But we train a man for facing them, not by locking him up in a monastery and stuffing him with wisdom and virtue, but by turning him loose on the stump. If he is a smart and enterprising fellow, which he usually is, he quickly discovers there that hooey pleases the boobs a great deal more than sense. Indeed, he finds that sense really disquiets and alarms them—that it makes them, at best, intolerably uncomfortable, just as a tight collar makes them uncomfortable, or a speck of dust in the eye, or the thought of Hell.

Ibid.

The worst of them is a great deal better company than most generals in the army, or writers of murder mysteries, or astrophysicists, and the best is a really superior and

83

wholly delightful man—full of sound knowledge, competent and prudent, frank and courageous, and quite as honest as any American can be without being clapped into a madhouse.

Ibid.

Will any of them venture to tell the plain truth, the whole truth and nothing but the truth about the situation of the country, foreign and domestic? Will any of them refrain from promises that he knows he can't fulfill—that no human being *could* fulfill? Will any of them utter a word, however obvious, that will alarm and alienate any of the huge packs of morons who clutter the public trough, wallowing in the pap that grows thinner and thinner, hoping against hope? Answer: maybe for a few weeks at the start. Maybe before the campaign really begins.

Ibid.

All politicians have read history; but one might say that they read it only in order to learn from it how to repeat the same calamities all over again.

PAUL VALÉRY (1871-1945)

The demagogue . . . is a good showman, whether at Nuremberg before a youth conference, or in Georgia at a political barbecue. He knows the tricks of the ham actor, the gestures, the tones of voice that can arouse passions. Always he dresses himself up as the little man, the common man come to life, grown to Brobdingnagian stature and become the "Duce" or the "Leader" or, maybe, "Ploughboy Pete."

ELLIS G. ARNALL: *The Shore Dimly Seen,* 1946

The Southern demagogue can no more leave the educational system alone than can his European equivalent. It is the nature of the demagogue. Reading and writing are the two enemies that he fears most....

Ibid.

Though I have been in politics for well over forty years, I loathe the professional politician. I have never been a regular. I have fought political machines and party politics at every opportunity.

FIORELLO LA GUARDIA (1882-1947):
The Making of an Insurgent, 1948

Why are congressmen called public servants? You never see servants that anxious to keep their jobs.

ROBERT QUILLEN (1887-1948)

The hazards of politics come not from campaigns and elections, as might be supposed, but rather from the nature of the creature that engages in politics. Ambition, love, jealousy, hate and the many emotions and reactions man is heir to frequently affect the course of nation and world more than principles or circumstances or events.

JAMES A. FARLEY: *The Sign,* August, 1948

The national elections of 1932 resulted in a Democratic land slide. Many Republican politicians who had held office for years lost their jobs and were cast adrift during a financial depression. As a practicing psychiatrist I chanced at that time to see a number of local politicians who suffered from mental breakdowns following their political defeat and I was astonished at the number of suicidal attempts and actual suicides among them. Here was food for thought. What was the matter with politicians as a group? Were they manic-depressive? Were they hypomanic? Were they constitutional inferiors? I have since had ample opportunity to ponder these questions and to study the problem in its broader aspects.

C. S. BLUEMEL (M.A., M.D., F.A.C.P., M.R.C.S.):
War, Politics and Insanity, 1948

It is evident that world security will never be attained under aggressive leadership . . . strife results not so much from a conflict of interests as from a conflict of personalities. In this conflict of personalities we find the stuff that wars are made of.

Ibid.

One of the cardinal causes of war, in the opinion of the present writer, is the fact that national leadership frequently falls to men of abnormal makeup. There are ill-balanced men of history who have been directed by a star of destiny, an inner voice, or a guiding light. Other men, free from hallucinations, have been motivated by hatred or suspicion having a paranoid quality. Still others have displayed delusions of grandeur in their political aspirations and wars of conquest. While some political leaders have been energized by a psychosis or mental illness, others have been afflicted with a less evident personality disorder but they have displayed pathological aggressiveness and obsessive-compulsive attitudes. These traits of personality may bring a man from obscurity to leadership and from leadership to dictatorship; they may at the same time bring

86

a country from peace to war. We shall study these aggressive and obsessive traits and we shall find a definite relationship between war, politics, and insanity.

Ibid.

Physicians examining prospective soldiers for the draft in World War II were cautioned to be on the lookout for five different types of mental disorder. No such precautions are taken with respect to national governing bodies. (Vide Medical Circular No. 1, National Headquarters, Selective Service System, 1940.)

Ibid.

In this volume is given an account, mostly derived from official sources, of the Bribery and Corruption that have prevailed in the island of Bombay from the dawn of history up to very near our own times. It is neither a congenial nor a pleasant task to sit down, write and compress within a small compass the story of the crooked ways of some Government servants and notables who had for so many centuries flourished in Bombay and found it a veritable Golconda not unlike their successors of the present generation.

> J. R. B. JEEJEEBHOY: Foreword to *Bribery and Corruption in Bombay: Being an historical Account From the Earliest to very Recent Times, of some Startling Cases of Illegal Gratification and other Misdemeanors in which were Criminally Involved High Dignitaries such as Governors, Deputy-Governors, Members of Council, Chief Justices, Judges, Commanders-in-Chief, Chief Mag-*

istrates, Advocate-Generals, Police Commis-
sioners, Collectors of Customs, Surgeons-
General, Commissioners, Chaplains, Editors,
and incidentally also Kings of Great Britain,
Governors-General of India and their Coun-
cillors, and other High Government Officials
and Private Individuals of Birth, Wealth &
Position. From Official Records, Old News-
papers and other Reliable Sources, 1952

The real test of the professional politician is his performance, not the passing "idols" or "ideals" to which he pays
temporary devotion. The ultimate sins are incompetency
in administration of public affairs and muddling in the
formulation of public policies.

JOSEPH H. BALL: Book preface, 1952

Few successful politicians are crusaders by nature. Very
often they march in parades, particularly the popular ones,
but rarely do they lead them.

Ibid.

... the great bulk of politicians are craftsmen and nothing more—bricklayers who build competently or incompe-
tently with the bricks or stones and according to the plans
specified by the architect—politics can be and often is an
art as well as a science. Politicians can be architects and
builders as well as mechanics. They can be gifted leaders
who help mold public opinion as well as follow it.

Ibid.

We shall have to fight the politician, who remembers only that the unborn have no votes and that since posterity has done nothing for us we need do nothing for posterity.

WILLIAM RALPH (DEAN) INGE (1860-1954)

Most statesmen have long noses. But I suppose that is very lucky, because most of them cannot see further than the length of them, so that a statesman with a short nose is handicapped by nature.

PAUL CLAUDEL (1868-1955)

A good politician is quite as unthinkable as an honest burglar.

H. L. MENCKEN (1880-1956)

Let us now look at who some criminoids are. In politics there are the demagogues and hate-mongers, those leaders and groups who seek gain at the expense of others. In present-day America, there often seems to be an affinity between politics and criminoid activity. Certainly, all of us know many men and women who, though apparently personally stable themselves, back demagogues who incite to acts of violence and hatred. All of us also know of public officials who use the cloak of authority to protect crime rings, "deals" and bribes. We also know that certain pressure groups may for their own gain favor inflation or depression or even war.

LEON J. SAUL, M.D.: *The Hostile Mind,* 1956

... the politician and bureaucrat are fair game for every shaft, the sacrificial kings to whom the Americans grant power but whom they reserve the right to stone to death.

The poorest, meanest, most misery-ridden fellow, the town drunk perhaps, the farmer ne'er-do-well, or the city derelict—can say anything, no matter how scurvy, about a man in public office.

MAX LERNER: *America as a Civilization,* 1957

After lots of people who go into politics have been in it for a while they find that to stay in politics they have to make all sorts of compromises to satisfy their supporters and that it becomes awfully important for them to keep their jobs because they have nowhere else to go.

ADLAI E. STEVENSON: Interview, 1958

When the issues involved are of no great weight the adults in control of a nation's policy are permitted . . . to behave like adults. But as soon as important economic interests or national prestige is involved, this grown-up Jekyll retires and his place is taken by an adolescent Hyde whose ethical standards are those of a boy gangster.

ALDOUS HUXLEY (1894-1963)

I have been associated, in one way or another over the years, with thousands of politicians in American Government, and I have yet to find among them a notable statesman. Yet each one, in all his mediocrity, fancies himself as God's answer to the people's prayers.

V. M. NEWTON, JR.: "Analysis of a Politician,"
Crusade for Democracy, 1961

The backward quality of Congress is readily apparent; so also are the reasons. It over-represents white farmers, hardly bothers with Southern Negroes at all, and makes a joke of affording fair representation to the 70 per cent of the population which is politically so misguided as to live in cities and suburbs.

DAVID T. BAZELON: *The Paper Economy*, 1963

The greatest asset a politician can have is a blameless record as far as women are concerned.

W. SOMERSET MAUGHAM (1874-1965):
Lord Mountdrago

A politician should have three hats. One for throwing in the ring, one for talking through, and one for pulling rabbits out of if elected.

CARL SANDBURG (1878-1967)

. . . there is a vital difference between the paranoid spokesman in politics and the clinical paranoiac: although they both tend to be overheated, oversuspicious, over-aggressive, grandiose, and apocalyptic in expression, the clinical paranoid sees the hostile and conspiratorial world in which he feels himself to be living as directed specifically against him; whereas the spokesman of the paranoid style finds it directed against a nation, a culture, a way of life whose fate affects not himself alone but millions of others.

RICHARD HOFSTADTER: *The Paranoid Style in American Politics*, 1965

In the history of New York City corruption, many millions of dollars have been passed to politicians and city officials by gangsters, vice rings and captains of industry.

MURRAY SCHUMACH: *New York Times*,
December 19, 1967; 53:1

Since politicians can never admit they have been wrong, they can only strive to find new and more acceptable ways of presenting obsolete doctrines.

PENDENNIS: *The Observer Review* (London), September 3,1967

When a man says he is an American politician, it is impossible not to suspect he is a swindler. Our politics is one education that no man can boast of and thereafter make it possible for anyone to trust him again . . . there should be an international convention forbidding any foreign student to study political science in the U.S.

MURRAY KEMPTON: *New York Post,* September 6, 1967

What successful advertising men, not to mention most politicians, understand clearly is that people will in fact do what is bad for them in the long run if offered a reward that can be collected in the short run. For this reason, neither the ad man nor the politician wastes much time reasoning with his constituents. He finds it more fruitfully spent at efforts to exploit their psychological motivations.

RUSSELL BAKER: *New York Times,* September 17, 1967

I think the man who is out of public life is a most fortunate person, for the reason that it is an era of intellectual dishonesty and hypocrisy.

JAMES M. COX (1870-   )

Politics is like roller skating. You go partly where you want to go, and partly where the damned things take you.

HENRY ASHURST (1874-   )

In fighting politicians you think you are winning and suddenly you find you have lost.

FIELD MARSHAL BERNARD L. MONTGOMERY
(1887-   )

Men play at being God, but lacking God's experience they wind up as politicians.

HARRY WILLIAM KING (1893-   )

A politician is an arse upon which every one has sat except a man.

E. E. CUMMINGS (1894-   ) : *A Politician*

America is the only country in the world where you can go on the air and kid politicians—and where politicians go on the air and kid the people.

GROUCHO MARX (1895-   )

The famous politician was trying to save both his faces.

JOHN GUNTHER (1901-   )

Democrats are to the manna born.

OGDEN NASH (1902-   ) : *Vive le Postmaster General*

The politician is a man who is sharply aware of men's disposition to docility and who exploits it systematically for the attainment of ends which he regards as good.

BERTRAND DE JOUVENEL (1903-   )

A politician is well qualified if his promises are, too.

HAROLD COFFIN

It is good business men that are corrupting our bad politicians.

JOSEPH W. FALK

Politicians act as though they thought the will of the people is a document bequeathing them something.

JOHN W. RAPER

Many an aspiring politician stakes his career on a few well-chosen wards.

ED WHITTAKER

In our social system the politician is able to reach a position of responsibility without having any training. He serves no apprenticeship. He masters no course of study. He need pass no examination as to his ability. He receives neither a diploma nor a license to practice. The veterinary who doctors our dogs and cats is required to show more careful preparation for his calling than is the politician who seeks to assume the right to direct not only our industrial but much of our personal life.

Author unidentified

When God gives a man an office, He gives him brains enough to fill it.

German proverb

As the bird feels about the net that entangles it so do men feel about those who rule them.

Chinese proverb

Common American Sayings about Politicians

A politician is a man with one hand full and the other open.

A practical politician shakes your hand before election and your acquaintance afterward.

In politics a man must learn to rise above principle.

In some African countries a man can't hold public office until he has shot a rhinoceros. In the United States a man is qualified if he can shoot the bull.

In political matters much may be said on both sides, and usually is.

It is less difficult to make a mark in politics than to erase one.

Many men go into politics with a fine future and come out with a terrible past.

One reason so many people are down on politicians is because they are so up on them.

People are blamed before they do wrong; politicians are extolled before they do right.

Politicians are animals who sit on a fence and keep both ears to the ground.

Politicians are people who have careers of a promising nature.

Politicians are persons of political cunning who, in opposition, know all the answers and, in office, curse the officials who cannot find them.

Politicians approach every question with an open mouth.

Politicians borrow your pot to cook your goose.

Politicians compare their own haloes and wings with rivals' horns and tails.

Politicians divide their time between running for office and running for cover.

Politicians get into the public eye by prying into the public chest.

Politicians go both ways when they come to the crossroads.

Politicians have what it takes to take what you've got.

Politicians, like poor relatives, are usually seen only when they need help.

Politicians love a wordy cause.

Politicians promise the people a car in every garage and after election put up parking meters.

Politicians spend half their time making laws and the other half helping campaign contributors evade them.

Politicians shake your hand before election and your confidence afterward.

Politicians shake your hand in the hope of shaking you down.

Politicians stand for what they think others will fall for.

Politicians succeed by playing both ends against the suckers.

Politicians talk in circles while standing foursquare.

There is no such thing as a cheap politician.

The unfunny thing about political jokes is that they often get elected and re-elected.

II

Of Politics

Power is precarious.
HERODOTUS: *Histories,* III, c. 430 B.C.

To the pair, body and soul, there correspond two arts—
that concerned with the soul I call the political art . . . in
the political art what corresponds to gymnastics [for the
body] is legislation while the counterpart of medicine [for
the body] is justice.

PLATO: *Gorgias*

Should we not then take in hand the tending of the city
and its citizens with the aim of making the citizens them-

selves as good as possible? For, as we discovered previously, without this there is no use in rendering any other kindly service, unless, that is to say, the thoughts of those who are to obtain much money and sovereignty or any other power whatever are good and noble.

PLATO: *Gorgias*

Again, all the other "works of politics" as one might call them—and there are many, for example, to make the people rich and free and without party spirit—all these things turned out to be neither good nor bad, but the necessary thing was to make them wise and to give them a share of knowledge, since knowledge was to be that which profited them and made them happy.

PLATO: *Euthydemus*

. . . whatever any state makes up its mind to enact as lawful for itself, really is lawful for it: in this field no individual or state is wiser than another. But where it is a question of laying down what is for its advantage or disadvantage, once more there, if anywhere, the theory will admit a difference between two advisers or between the decision of two different states in respect of truth, and would hardly venture to assert that any enactment which a state supposes to be for its advantage will quite certainly be so.

PLATO: *Theaetetus*

A citizen has already a calling which will make full demands on him, in view of the constant practice and wide study it involves, in the preservation and enjoyment of the

100

public social order—a task which permits of no relegation to the second place.

PLATO: *Laws,* VIII

I wonder why the great men of the past . . . did not take an active part in politics.

PLATO: *Greater Hippias*

Your countrymen are right in admitting the tinker and cobbler to advise about politics.

PLATO: *Protagoras*

That common doctrine which is over them all, and guards the laws, and all things that are in the state, and truly weaves them all into one, if we could describe under a name characteristic of this common nature, most truly we may call politics.

PLATO: *Statesman*

When the foundation of politics is in the letter only and in custom, and knowledge is divorced from action, can we wonder at the miseries that are there, and always will be, in states?

Ibid.

The good of man must be the goal of the science of politics.

ARISTOTLE: *The Nichomachean Ethics,* I, c. 340 B.C.

Democracy arose from men thinking that if they are equal in any respect they are equal in all respects.

ARISTOTLE: *Politics*

A democracy, when put to the strain, grows weak, and is supplanted by oligarchy.

ARISTOTLE: *Rhetoric,* **I**

Monarchy degenerates into tyranny, aristocracy into oligarchy, and democracy into savage violence and anarchy.

POLYBIUS: *Histories,* V, 125 B.C.

When a state increases in wealth and luxury men indulge in ambitious projects and are eager for high dignities. Each feels ashamed that any of his fellow men should surpass him. The common people feel themselves oppressed by the grasping of some and their vanity is flattered by others. Fired with evil passions, they are no longer willing to submit to control, but demand that everything be subject to their authority. The invariable result is that the government assumes the noble names of free and popular, but becomes in fact that most execrable thing, mob rule.

*Ibid.,*VI

Some have said that it is not the business of private men to meddle with government—a bold and dishonest saying, which is fit to come from no mouth but that of a tyrant or a slave. To say that private men have nothing to do with government is to say that private men have nothing to do with their own happiness or misery; that people ought not to concern themselves whether they be naked or clothed, fed or starved, deceived or instructed, protected or destroyed.

MARCUS PORCIUS CATO (95-46 B.C.)

The office makes the man.

Latin proverb

Nothing is more foreign to us Christians than politics.
TERTULLIAN: *The Christian's Defence,* c. 215

People's voice is God's voice, men say.
THOMAS HOCCLEVE (c. 1370-c. 1450); *De Regimine
Principum,* 104

Men ought either to be indulged or utterly destroyed,
for if you merely offend them they take vengeance, but if
you injure them greatly they are unable to retaliate, so that
the injury done to a man ought to be such that vengeance
cannot be feared.
NICCOLO MACHIAVELLI: *The Prince,* III, 1513

Severities should be dealt out all at once, so that their
suddenness may give less offence; benefits ought to be
handed out drop by drop, so that they may be relished the
more.
Ibid., VIII

If the chief party, whether it be people, or army, or
nobility, which you think most useful and of most consequence to you for the conservation of your dignity, be corrupt, you must follow their humor and indulge them, and
in that case honesty and virtue are pernicious.
Ibid., XIX

The world is ruled by a certain few, even as a little boy
of twelve rules, governs, and keeps a hundred big and
strong oxen in a pasture.
MARTIN LUTHER: *Table Talk,* CLVII, 1569

O, that estates, degrees, and offices
Were not deriv'd corruptly, and that clear honor
Were purchased by the merit of the wearer!

> WILLIAM SHAKESPEARE: *The Merchant of
> Venice,* II, 1600

Political rule is so natural and necessary to the human race that it cannot be withdrawn without destroying nature herself; for the nature of man is such that he is a social animal.

> ST. ROBERT BELLARMINE (1542-1627): *De Laicis,* 5

Political power, considered in general, not descending in particular to monarchy, aristocracy, or democracy, comes directly from God alone. . . .

> *Ibid.,* 6

All empire is no more than pow'r in trust.

> JOHN DRYDEN: *Absalom and Achitophel,* 1682

They who possess the prince [politician] possess the laws.

> *Ibid.,* I

Plots, true or false, are necessary things,
To raise up commonwealths, and ruin kings.

> *Ibid.*

To die for faction is a common evil.

> *Ibid.,* II

'Tis not juggling that is to be blamed, but much juggling, for the world cannot be governed without it.

> JOHN SELDEN: *Table Talk,* 1689

The great question which, in all ages, has disturbed mankind, and brought on them the greatest part of those mischiefs which have ruined cities, depopulated countries, and disordered the peace of the world, has been, not whether there be power in the world, nor whence it came, but who should have it.

JOHN LOCKE: *Treatise on Government,* I, 1690

State-Business is a cruel Trade; Good-nature is a Bungler in it.

LORD HALIFAX (1633-1695)

The best Party is but a kind of Conspiracy against the rest of the Nation.

LORD HALIFAX

Ignorance maketh most Men go into a Party, and Shame keepeth them from getting out of it.

LORD HALIFAX

CORRUPT MINISTERS The Cause of Publick CA-LAMITIES; Or, The Interest of the King and his People, One. Being a Brief Relation of some Publick Crimes Committed in the Government, during the Late WAR. Humbly offer'd to the Consideration of the Honourable House of Commons.

ROBERT CROSFIELD: London, 1701

Politics, as the word is commonly understood, are nothing but corruptions.

JONATHAN SWIFT: *Thoughts on Various Subjects,* 1706

You see, in elections for members to sit in Parliament, how far saluting rows of old women, drinking with clowns, and being upon a level with the lower part of mankind in that wherein they themselves are lowest, their diversions, will carry a candidate.

RICHARD STEELE: *The Spectator,* April 4, 1712

Politics is not the Business of a Woman.

MARY MANLEY: *The Adventures of Rivella,* 1714

Party-spirit at best is but the madness of many for the gain of a few.

ALEXANDER POPE: *Letter to Martha Blount,* 1714

Party is the madness of many, for the gain of a few.

ALEXANDER POPE: *Thoughts on Many Subjects*

All political parties die at last of swallowing their own lies.

JOHN ARBUTHNOT (1667-1735): *Epigram,* 1735

Confound their politics,
Frustrate their knavish tricks.

HENRY CAREY (c. 1693-1743): *God Save the King*

The tumultuous love of the populace must be seized and enjoyed in its first transports; there is no hoarding it to use upon occasions; it will not keep.

LORD CHESTERFIELD: Letters, 1748

Republics end through luxury, monarchies through poverty.

CHARLES DE SECONDAT DE MONTESQUIEU: *The Spirit of the Laws,* VII, 1748

'Tis a political maxim that all government tends to despotism, and like the human frame brings at its birth the latent seed which finally shall destroy the constitution. This is a melancholy truth—but such is the lot of humanity.

JOSIAH QUINCY, JR.: Letter to
Boston Gazette, 1767

There is a holy mistaken zeal in politics as well as religion. By persuading others, we convince ourselves.

JUNIUS: *Letters*, 1769

Power is always gradually stealing away from the many to the few, because the few are more vigilant and consistent.

SAMUEL JOHNSON (1709-1784): *Adventurer*,
c. 1753-1754

Why, Sir, most schemes of political improvement are very laughable things.

SAMUEL JOHNSON: *Boswell's Life*, II, 1769

Politics are now nothing more than the means of rising in the world.

SAMUEL JOHNSON: *Boswell's Life*, 1775

Conscience has no more to do with gallantry than it has with politics.

RICHARD BRINSLEY SHERIDAN: *The Duenna*, 1775

Magnanimity in politics is not seldom the truest wisdom; and a great empire and little minds go ill together.

EDMUND BURKE: *On Conciliation with America*,
1775

I must not write a word to you about politics, because you are a woman.

JOHN ADAMS: Letter to his wife, 1779

A time like this, a busy, bustling time,
Suits ill with writers, very ill with rhyme;
Unheard we sing, when party-rage runs strong,
And mightier madness checks the flowing song.

GEORGE CRABBE: *The Newspaper,* 1785

Faction seldom leaves a man honest, however it might find him.

SAMUEL JOHNSON: *Works,* 1787

There are few minds to which tyranny is not delightful.

SAMUEL JOHNSON: *Letters*

All political power is a trust.

JAMES FOX: Speech, 1788

There is scarcely anything more harmless than political or party malice. It is best to leave it to itself. Opposition and contradiction are the only means of giving it life or duration.

JOHN WITHERSPOON (1723-1794)

That base business of electioneering. . . .

JEDIDIAH MORSE:
American Geography, I, 472, 1795

Men still have to be governed by deception.

G. C. LICHTENBERG: *Reflections,* 1799

Politics. The art of governing mankind by deceiving them.

ISAAC D'ISRAELI: *Curiosities of Literature*, c. 1800

Politics is such a torment that I would advise every one I love not to mix with it.

THOMAS JEFFERSON:
Letter to Martha Jefferson Randolph, 1800

Government has hardened into a tyrannical monopoly, and the human race in general becomes as absolutely property as beasts in the plow.

JOHN DICKINSON:
Letter to Thomas McKean, 1802

The politics of courts are so mean that private people would be ashamed to act in the same way; all is trick and finesse, to which the common cause is sacrificed.

LORD NELSON (1758-1805)

Power, like a desolating pestilence,
Pollutes whate'er it touches.

PERCY BYSSHE SHELLEY: *Queen Mab,* III, 1813

While all other sciences have advanced, that of government is at a standstill—little better understood, little better practised now than three or four thousand years ago.

JOHN ADAMS: Letter to Thomas Jefferson, 1813

I consider the government [of England] as the most flagitious which has existed since the days of Philip of Macedon, whom they make their model. It is not only founded in corruption itself, but insinuates the same poison into the bowels of every other, corrupts its councils, nourishes factions, stirs up revolutions, and places its own happiness in fomenting commotions and civil wars among others, thus rendering itself truly the *hostis humani generis.*

THOMAS JEFFERSON: Letter to John Adams, 1816

It is safest to be moderately base—to be flexible in shame, and to be always ready for what is generous, good, and just, when anything is to be gained by virtue.

SYDNEY SMITH
Letter to the Electors on the Catholic Question, 1826

In politics experiments mean revolutions.

BENJAMIN DISRAELI: *Popanilla,* IV, 1827

In politics, what begins in fear usually ends in folly.

SAMUEL T. COLERIDGE: *Table Talk,* 1830

Vain hope, to make people happy by politics!

THOMAS CARLYLE: *Journal,* October 10, 1831

I hate all bungling as I do sin, but particularly bungling in politics, which leads to the misery and ruin of many thousands and millions of people.

JOHANN WOLFGANG VON GOETHE (1749-1832)

I hold them [politics] to be subject to laws as fixed as matter itself, and to be as fit a subject for the application of the highest intellectual power.

JOHN C. CALHOUN: *Senate Speech,* 1833

Government has come to be a trade, and is managed solely on commercial principles. A man plunges into politics to make his fortune, and only cares that the world shall last his days.

RALPH WALDO EMERSON:
Letter to Thomas Carlyle, 1835

In politics, as in religion, there are devotees who show their reverence for a departed saint by converting his tomb into a sanctuary for crime.

T. B. MACAULAY: *Sir James Mackintosh,* 1835

War is nothing but the continuation of politics by other means.

GENERAL KARL VON CLAUSEWITZ (1780-1831):
On War, Preface *et seq.* (1832-1837)

Nothing is politically right which is morally wrong.

DANIEL O'CONNELL (1775-1847)

Political power is merely the organized power of one class to oppress another.

KARL MARX and FRIEDRICH ENGELS:
The Communist Manifesto, 1848

The executive of the modern state is but a committee for managing the common affairs of the bourgeoisie. [Often rendered as: The state is the executive committee of the ruling class.]

Ibid.

Democracies are prone to war, and war consumes them.

WILLIAM H. SEWARD:
Eulogy on John Quincy Adams, 1848

How does it become a man to behave towards the American government today? I answer, that he cannot without disgrace be associated with it.

HENRY D. THOREAU:
An Essay on Civil Disobedience, 1849

To be governed is to be watched, inspected, spied upon, directed, law-ridden, regulated, penned up, indoctrinated, preached at, checked, appraised, seized, censured, commanded, by beings who have neither title, knowledge, nor virtue. To be governed is to have every operation, every transaction, every movement noted, registered, counted, rated, stamped, measured, numbered, assessed, licensed, refused, authorized, indorsed, admonished, prevented, reformed, redressed, corrected.

PIERRE JOSEPH PROUDHON:
Confessions d'un Revolutionaire, 1849

Whoever lays his hand on me to govern me is a usurper and tyrant, and I declare him my enemy.

Ibid.

There is a certain satisfaction in coming down to the lowest ground of politics, for we get rid of cant and hypocrisy.

RALPH WALDO EMERSON:
Representative Men, VI, 1850

Politics is but the common pulse-beat, of which revolution is the fever-spasm.

WENDELL PHILLIPS: Speech to the
Massachusetts Anti-Slavery Society, Boston, 1853

In politics there is no honor.

BENJAMIN DISRAELI: *Vivien Grey,* IV, 1853

In politics nothing is contemptible.

Ibid.

Finality is not the language of politics.

BENJAMIN DISRAELI:
Speech, House of Commons, 1859

There is no gambling like politics.

BENJAMIN DISRAELI

A majority is always better than the best repartee.

BENJAMIN DISRAELI

Politics is the science of exigencies.

THEODORE PARKER (1810-1860)

Politics is a deleterious profession, like some poisonous handicrafts. Men in power have no opinions, but may be had cheap for any opinion, for any purpose.

RALPH WALDO EMERSON:
The Conduct of Life, 1860

Every actual State is corrupt. Good men must not obey the laws too well. What satire on government can equal the

113

severity of censure conveyed in the word *politics* which now for ages has signified *cunning,* intimating that the State is a trick?

RALPH WALDO EMERSON: *Journals* (1861-1865)

Democracy becomes a government of bullies tempered by editors.

Ibid., VII, 193 (1913 ed.)

The imbecility of man is always inviting the impudence of power.

RALPH WALDO EMERSON: *Works,* I, 365 (1913 ed.)

The punishment which the wise suffer, who refuse to take part in the government, is to live under the government of worse men.

RALPH WALDO EMERSON

Concentration is the secret of strength in politics, in war, in trade, in short in all management of human affairs.

RALPH WALDO EMERSON

But political checks will no more act of themselves, than a bridle will direct a horse without a rider.

JOHN STUART MILL: *Representative Government,* 1861

What is called politics is comparatively so superficial and inhuman, that, practically, I have never fairly recognized that it concerns me at all.

HENRY D. THOREAU (1817-1862)

Politics . . . are but the cigar smoke of a man.

HENRY D. THOREAU

Politics is the gizzard of society, full of grit and gravel, and the two political parties are its two opposite halves— sometimes split into quarters—which grind on each other. Not only individuals, but states, have thus a confirmed dyspepsia.

HENRY D. THOREAU: *Life Without Principle,* 1863

Politics is not an exact science.

OTTO VON BISMARCK:' Speech, Prussian Upper House, 1863

A Parliament is nothing less than a big meeting of more or less idle people.

WALTER BAGEHOT: *The English Constitution,* 1867

Politics makes strange bedfellows. [Later variant: If politics makes strange bedfellows sex makes even stranger ones.]

C. E. WARNER:' *My Summer in a Garden,* XV, 1870

All political questions, all matters of right, are at bottom only questions of might.

AUGUST BEBEL: Speech in Reichstag, 1871

Even in the purest democracies, such as the United States and Switzerland, a privileged minority stands against the vast enslaved majority.

MIKHAIL A. BAKUNIN: *Dieu et l'État,* 1871

A Congressional appropriation costs money. Just reflect, for instance. A majority of the House committee, say $10,000 apiece—$40,000; a majority of the Senate committee, the same each—say $40,000; a little extra to one or two chairmen of one or two such committees, say $10,000 each—$20,000; and there's $100,000 of the money gone, to begin with. Then, seven male lobbyists, at $3,000 each—$21,000; one female lobbyist, $10,000; a high moral Congressman or Senator here and there—the high moral ones cost more, because they give tone to a measure—say ten of these at $3,000 each, is $30,000; then a lot of small-fry country members who won't vote for anything whatever without pay. . . .

President of the Columbus River
Slackwater Navigation Company in
MARK TWAIN: *The Gilded Age,* 1873

In any single "first-class" hotel in Washington, at any time during midsession, at least half a dozen of these lobbyesses are thus at work at once, each one roping in her dozen or ten of wild-cat Congressmen. The lever of lust is used to pry up more legislators to the sticking point than money itself avails to seduce.

EDWARD WINSLOW MARTIN: *Behind the Scenes in Washington,* 1873

When the day comes on which it will be considered as disgraceful to be seen in a caucus as to be seen in a gambling house or brothel, then my interest will wake up again and legitimate politics will get a new birth.

HENRY ADAMS:
Letter to Henry Cabot Lodge, June 24, 1876

Politics are a very unsatisfactory game.

HENRY ADAMS:
Letter to Charles Milnes Gaskell, March 26, 1874

The political field is amusing though somewhat saddening to the believer in human perfectability.

HENRY ADAMS:
Letter to Henry Cabot Lodge, August 31, 1876

Both parties are impossibly corrupt and the public thoroughly indifferent.

HENRY ADAMS:
Letter to Charles Milnes Gaskell, September 8, 1876

I never refuse. I never contradict. I sometimes forget.

BENJAMIN DISRAELI: Explaining his successful dealings with Queen Victoria, 1877

In politics it is necessary to take nothing tragically and everything seriously.

LOUIS ADOLPHE THIERS (1797-1877)

All government is evil.

B. R. HAYDON: *Table Talk,* 1876

I always voted at my party's call,
And I never thought of thinking for myself at all.

W. S. GILBERT: *H. M. S. Pinafore,* 1878

The way to have power is to take it.

WILLIAM MARCY TWEED (1823-1878), Tammany Boss

. . . practical politics [is] . . . the politics of the coming election.

WILLIAM E. GLADSTONE: *Speech,* Dalkeith, 1879

She had got to the bottom of this business of democratic government and found out that it was nothing more than government of any other kind.

HENRY ADAMS: *Democracy,* 1880

Real politics are the possession and distribution of power.

BENJAMIN DISRAELI: *Endymion,* 1880

Politics is perhaps the only profession for which no preparation is thought necessary.

ROBERT LOUIS STEVENSON:
Familiar Studies of Men and Books, V, 1882

We should all be glad if we could step aside and say: "Now let us have a day of rest. Politics are over and the millennium is begun." But we live in a world of sin and sorrow.

THOMAS B. REED: Speech, Philadelphia, 1884

If you do not know how to lie, cheat and steal, turn your attention to politics and learn.

JOSH BILLINGS (H. W. Shaw) (1818-1885)

[As to women lobbyists] Some of them were the widows of officers of the army or navy, others the daughters of Congressmen, and others had drifted from home localities where they had found themselves the subject of scandalous comments. The parlors of some of these dames were exquisitely furnished with works of art and bric-a-brac, donated by admirers. Every evening they received, and in the winter their blazing wood fires were surrounded by a distinguished circle. Some would treat favored guests to a game of euchre, and as midnight approached there was always an adjournment to the dining-room, where a choice supper was served. . . . Who could blame the Congressman for leaving the bad cooking of his hotel or boardinghouse, with an absence of home comforts, to walk into the parlor which the adroit spider lobbyist had cunningly woven for him?

BEN PERLEY POORE: *Perley's Reminiscences of Sixty Years in the National Metropolis,* II, 1886

The strife of politics tends to unsettle the calmest understanding, and ulcerate the most benevolent heart. There are no bigotries or absurdities too gross for parties to create or adopt under the stimulus of political passions.

EDWIN PERCY WHIPPLE (1819-1886)

Politics are a gambling casino in which the spectators pay as much as the players.

DESIRE NISARD (1806-1888)

We all know what Parliament is, and we are all ashamed of it.

ROBERT LOUIS STEVENSON: *Ethical Studies*

The results of political changes are hardly ever those which their friends hope or their foes fear.

THOMAS HENRY HUXLEY: *Government,* 1890

119

Democracy means simply the bludgeoning of the people by the people for the people.

OSCAR WILDE:
The Soul of Man Under Socialism, 1891

Politics are a part of morals.
HENRY EDWARD (CARDINAL) MANNING (1808-1892)

Public office is a public trust.

DEMOCRATIC PARTY
NATIONAL PLATFORM, 1892

Power feeds on its spoils, and dies when its victims refuse to be despoiled. They can't persuade it to death; they can't vote it to death; they can't shoot it to death, but they can always starve it to death.
BENJAMIN R. RUCKER: *Instead of a Book,* 1893

Women are said to be the most active and successful lobbyists in Washington.
JAMES, LORD BRYCE: *The American Commonwealth,* I, 1893

In a Republican district I was a Republican. In a Democratic district, I was a Democrat. And in a doubtful district I was doubtful. But I was always for Erie.
JAY GOULD, *chief owner of the Erie Railroad*

The old political wire-pullers never go near the man they want to gain, if they can help it; they find out who his intimates and managers are, and work through them. Always handle any positively charged electrical body, whether it is charged with passion or power, with some nonconductor between you and it, not with naked hands.

OLIVER WENDELL HOLMES (1809-1894)

The spoils system, that practice which turns public offices, high and low, from public trusts into objects of prey and booty for the victorious party, may without extravagance of language be called one of the greatest criminals in our history, if not the greatest. In the whole catalogue of our ills there is none more dangerous to the vitality of our free institutions.

CARL SCHURZ: Speech, Chicago, December 12, 1894

. . . suspect power more than vice. . . .

LORD ACTON: Inaugural lecture on
The Study of History, June 11, 1895

Politics is mostly pill-taking.

THOMAS B. REED, Speaker of the House of
Representatives: Letter to John Dalzell, 1896

Never vote for a tax bill nor against an appropriation bill.

American political maxim

Be polite. Write diplomatically. Even in a declaration of war one observes the rules of politeness.

OTTO VON BISMARCK (1815-1898)

Politics is the doctrine of the possible, the attainable.

OTTO VON BISMARCK

Politics is the art of the next best.

OTTO VON BISMARCK

The Decalogue and the Golden Rule have no place in a political campaign, and purity in politics is an iridescent dream.

JOHN J. INGALLS (1833-1900)

The field of politics always presents the same struggle. There are the Right and the Left, and in the middle is the Swamp. The Swamp is made up of know-nothings, of them who are without ideas, of them who are always with the majority.

AUGUST BEBEL: Speech to the Dresden Congress of the Social-Democratic Party, 1903

In politics you can't be true to all of your friends all of the time.

PERRY S. HEATH (1857-1927), secretary of the Republican National Committee, 1900-1904

At the beginning of the 19th century "The oft-vaunted freedom of the [British] electorate—an essential principle of the Constitution—was in practice inhibited by three major influences: the political ignorance and indifference of the vast majority of those living in a stratified society where only the upper classes could legislate and rule; the traditional right of certain members of these classes—the great landowners in the counties and the patrons in most boroughs—to dictate the elector's choice; and the traditional relationship between member and constituents based

122

on the theory that since the vote was a marketable commodity the member must look after his supporters. From the point of view of the electorate as a whole the privilege of the franchise was conceived in terms of personal advantage in the narrowest sense.

CORNELIUS O'LEARY: *The Elimination of Corrupt Practices in British Elections: 1868-1911*, 1962

The earliest examples of electoral bribery were of a negative type—agreements between burgesses and their constituents to serve for less than the statutory rate of wages, or to accept less than their statutory travelling expense allowance. . . . Gradually, as the two Houses developed their distinctive character, seats in the Lower House came to be valued by the merchants, lawyers, and county squires—to whom the restrictive laws of the fifteenth century had virtually confined Parliamentary representation. . . . The conditions were soon present for the effective exercise of positive bribery, treating and intimidation or undue influence. . . . In the reign of Elizabeth I great noblemen (such as the Earl of Essex) could dictate their choice to the small corporations. . . . Bribery was from the beginning the characteristic vice of borough elections. Treating, intimidation, and undue influence arose in the counties, where the electorates were much larger. . . . Fraudulent returns by sheriffs were also among the earlier corrupt practices mentioned in statutes. . . . Yet all these penalties and procedures did not prevent sheriffs from altering the returns and devising various expedients to get favoured candidates elected—and their own fees paid too.

... Throughout the seventeenth century money bribes and treating increased with the competition for seats. . . . Borough corporations were by now openly selling the seats to wealthy candidates and charging fees for admission to the freedom where that was a condition of memberships. . . . All the practices mentioned above were becoming diversified: candidates were expected to support local industries, build roads and bridges, provide a water supply, and generally to "do something for the Corporation." . . . The growing cost of elections, resulting from the competition to get seats in the House of Commons, caused votes to be regarded as marketable commodities with fluctuating, but generally appreciating, values. . . . It also tended to drive out of the Commons the small country squires and merchants, replacing them by plutocrats, "Nabobs," and "Carribbees," and encouraged place-hunting. . . . The price of seats was regulated by the demands of the market. . . . The penalties in the Act of 1729 were severe but were applied only occasionally. . . . These measures, however, were merely scratching the surface of electoral corruption. . . . The purchase of electoral power went on at all levels of the system: nomination boroughs were purchased outright from the proprietors, or leased for a period; boroughs with electorates that could not be controlled were won over by the annual dinner and septennial bribe (where the quirks of the system allowed the voters to be poor and ill-educated), or by the more discerning gifts and favours where the wealthy capital burgesses or burgageholders had the deciding voice. . . . Treating too increased in the decades after Reform. . . . Violence or intimidation was also common at this period. . . . During these decades the

124

attention of the House of Commons was frequently directed to the prevalence of corrupt practices and the inadequacy of the existing laws. . . .

Ibid., I

The moral revulsion against these practices came at much the same time as the revulsion against drunkenness. Political consciousness also struggled forth: elections not only lost their corrupt aspects but also much of their colour and their festive character. The exercise of the franchise was at last regarded as a solemn duty, a right of citizenship but also a responsibility. When all is said, however, it was the members of the House of Commons who from first to last set the moral tone, unprompted by outside pressure groups. At the cost of personal sacrifice to some of its members Parliament managed within one generation to sweep away traditions that were centuries old and were regarded by many as wellnigh ineradicable. It is an achievement of which any legislature might well be proud.

Ibid., Conclusions

Politics. The conduct of public affairs for private advantage.

AMBROSE BIERCE: *The Devil's Dictionary,* 1906

Power tends to corrupt, and absolute power corrupts absolutely. Great men are almost always bad men. . . .

LORD ACTON: *Historical Essays and Studies,* 1907

Modern politics is, at bottom, a struggle not of men but of forces. The men become every year more and more creatures of force, massed about central powerhouses. The conflict is no longer between the men, but between the motors that drive the men, and the men tend to succumb to their own motive forces.

HENRY ADAMS:
The Education of Henry Adams, 1907

In politics, strangely enough, the best way to play your cards is to lay them face upwards on the table.

H. G. WELLS: *New Worlds for Old,* 1908

At present politics is the only instrumentality through which moral and economic truths may be translated into the life of the people. Instead of being, as it should be, only the agency, the means, to that end, which is the common welfare, modern politics has become an end in itself, this end being office and the ever-increasing perquisites of office. I want this book to show the perverted character of modern politics.

LYNN HAINES: *Your Congress,* 1915

Politics I conceive to be nothing more than the science of the ordered progress of society along the lines of greatest usefulness and convenience to itself.

WOODROW WILSON
Speech, Washington, January 6, 1916

Practical politics consists in ignoring facts.

HENRY ADAMS (1838-1918)

The whole aim of practical politics is to keep the populace alarmed (and hence clamorous to be led to safety) by an endless series of hobgoblins.

H. L. MENCKEN: *In Defence of Women,* 1923

Politics are always a struggle for power, disguised and modified by prudence, reason and moral pretext.

WILLIAM HURRELL MALLOCK (1849-1923)

In politics the choice is constantly between two evils.

JOHN MORLEY (1838-1923)

There are no morals in politics; there is only expedience. A scoundrel may be of use to us just because he is a scoundrel.

V. I. LENIN (1870-1924)

Politics is economics in action.

ROBERT M. LA FOLLETTE (1855-1925)

If you wish the sympathy of broad masses then you must tell them the crudest and most stupid things.

ADOLPH HITLER: *Mein Kampf,* 1925

Politics under democracy consists almost wholly of the discovery, chase and scotching of bugaboos. The statesman becomes, in the last analysis, a mere witch-hunter, a glorified smeller and snooper, eternally chanting "Fe, Fi, Fo, Fum!" It has been so in the United States since the earliest days. The whole history of the country has been a history of melodramatic pursuits of horrendous monsters, some of them imaginary: the red-coats, the Hessians, the

127

monocrats, again the red-coats, the Bank, the Catholics, Simon Legree, the Slave Power, Jeff Davis, Mormonism, Wall Street, the rum demon, John Bull, the hell hounds of plutocracy, the trusts, General Weyler, Pancho Villa, German spies, hyphenates, the Kaiser, Bolshevism. The list might be lengthened indefinitely; a complete chronicle of the Republic could be written in terms of it, and without omitting a single important episode.

H. L. MENCKEN: *Notes on Democracy,* 1926

Government under democracy is thus government by orgy, almost by orgasm.

Ibid.

Public policies are determined and laws are made by small minorities playing upon the fears and imbecilities of the mob—sometimes minorities of intelligent and honest men, but usually minorities of rogues.

Ibid.

. . . the great masses of Americans to-day . . . actually look for leading to professional politicians, who are influenced in turn by small but competent and determined minorities, with special knowledge and special interests. It was thus that the plain people were shoved into the late war, and it is thus that they will be shoved into the next one.

Ibid.

The American people, true enough, are sheep. Worse, they are donkeys. Yet worse, to borrow from their own dialect, they are goats. They are thus constantly bam-

128

boozled and exploited by small minorities of their own number, by determined and ambitious individuals, and even by exterior groups. The business of victimizing them is a lucrative profession, an exact science, and a delicate and lofty art. It has its masters and it has its quacks. Its lowest reward is a seat in Congress or a job as a Prohibition agent, i.e., a licensed blackleg; its highest reward is immortality.

Ibid.

A democratic state, indeed, is so firmly grounded upon cheats and humbugs of all sorts that they inevitably colour its dealings with other nations, and so one always finds it regarded as a dubious friend and a tricky foe. That the United States, in its foreign relations, has descended to gross deceits and tergiversations since the earliest days of the Republic was long ago pointed out by Lecky; it is regarded universally to-day as a pious fraud—which is to say, as a Puritan. Nor has England, the next most eminent democratic state, got the name of *perfide Albion* for nothing. Ruled by shady men, a nation itself becomes shady.

Ibid.

The science of politics under the democracy consists in trading with them [the masses], i.e., in hoodwinking and swindling them. In return for what they want, or for the mere appearance of what they want, they yield up what the politician wants, and what the enterprising minorities behind him want. The bargaining is conducted to the tune of affecting rhetoric, with music by the choir, but it is as simple and sordid at bottom as the sale of a mule. It lies quite outside the bounds of honour, and even of common decency. It is a combat betwen jackals and jackasses. It is the master transaction of democratic states.

Ibid.

All observers of democracy, from Tocqueville to the Adams brothers and Wilfred Scawen Blunt, have marveled at its corruptions on the political side, and speculated heavily as to the causes thereof. . . . Gentz, who served Metternich . . . contended that the introduction of democracy on the Continent would bring in a reign of bribery, and thus destroy the integrity and authority of the State.

Ibid.

The government is mainly an expensive organization to regulate evildoers, and tax those who behave; government does little for fairly respectable people except annoy them.

EDGAR WATSON HOWE: *Notes for My Biographer,* 1926

Politics, the servant, the incidental thing, has grown so great as to overshadow and subordinate all else in American public life. It has become a business, as thoroughly monopolized as any industrial trust. It is unaltruistic. It is selfish to the last degree. It is lawless to the point of anarchy. It has become the mightiest, most ruthless revolutionary force that exists.

LYNN HAINES: *Your Servants in the Senate,* 1926

Because predatory interest, knowing the dollars and cents meaning of government and dependent upon special privileges, through control of public opinion and lavish campaign contributions, can accomplish more for end-in-itself politics than can the electorate, this ruling caste power has formed a partnership with the great industrial and financial interests. The objectives of this partnership are not issues of public welfare, but the selfish results of dominance, measured in spoils for the politician and privileges for the profiteer.

Ibid.

This new kind of ruling caste power, through a cleverly contrived and manipulated control of politics, can and does sell to the highest bidder the people's most priceless possession—the favors of government. Without any semblance of ownership, nor even a brokerage interest, professional politicians barter away the public welfare.

Ibid.

There was an orgy of corruption in our public life—indescribably vicious and brazen. The oil scandals were but a small part of it. War graft was rampant—on a gigantic scale, and without a single big successful prosecution. What happened to alien property funds would probably make many millionaires. Yet, through all this period of lying and stealing, there was a public apathy terrifying to those of us who love our country and desire its perpetuity as "a free government." Even as flagrant a prostitution as Newberryism aroused little popular resentment—so completely has the conscience of the American people been chloroformed by propaganda. Think of it! An atmosphere of the worst criminality in high public places, and hardly a protest from the people! Nobody in the penitentiary, nor likely to be! Yet the people felt no impulse to

131

"clean house"; instead they seemed to acquiesce in the persecution of whoever raised voice or hand to purge America of its deadliest enemies. So all-powerful is propaganda that today Abraham Lincoln would not be possible. . . . He would be attacked from every angle.

Ibid.

Oil had a room in an office building and presumed to summon potential presidential and vice-presidential candidates to that room where men good-naturedly discussed our foreign relations with Mexico in the oral examination which was given to those whom oil was about to bless with its support. . . . There can be no doubt in the mind of anyone who reads the testimony in the numerous suits brought later by the Government, that oil control led the [Republican] convention of 1920. It worked through the Senate cabal, led by the irreconcilables who were so busy hating Wilson that they became easy victims of the greed for oil.

WILLIAM ALLEN WHITE: *Masks in a Pageant,* 1928

. . . in politics a certain amount of corruption is inevitable and inescapable. Purity in politics is an impractical dream.

FRANK R. KENT: *Political Behavior,* 1928

Here is a game without recognized standards, rules or requirements, open to the worst as well as to the best, with an almost uncountable number of prizes ranging from the most powerful and important office in the world—the Presidency—to the $2 bill eagerly sought by the venal voter on election day.

Ibid.

The truth is that in politics both as to means and methods, every man goes just as far in compromising with rigid virtue as his individual character will permit. In some cases this means that there is really no limit; in others it means going only a little way, but the difference is merely in degree. . . .

Ibid.

One of the most curious things about politics in America is the extraordinary lack of knowledge concerning its practice and principles not only on the part of the people as a whole but of the practitioners themselves.

Ibid.

Insincerity in politics is an essential part of a political equipment but it is harmful if too baldly exposed.

Ibid.

. . . the great mass of the voters have no inherent or instinctive objection to corruption; that at heart, however they may have felt in former decades, they do not now expect or demand rigid honesty in public officials, party leaders or party candidates.

Ibid.

When times are good, work is plenty and wages high, they [the voters] look upon corruption in public office with a curious degree of tolerance and complacency. Under such conditions they regard the charges of crookedness coming from the outs against the ins a natural thing to be expected, as part of the game. The disposition down in the precincts

is to believe that of course the ins are grafting a little, but
so will the outs when they get in—it is what they all do.
Ibid.

Politics makes strange postmasters.
FRANK McKINNEY "KIN" HUBBARD (1868-1930)

Politics are a business—at least they are a field in which
experience tells for usefulness and effectiveness—and a
man who has devoted his entire life to the successful estab-
lishment of a business is generally not the man who will be
useful to the public in the administration of public business.
WILLIAM HOWARD TAFT (1857-1930)

[There is the] utter inability of emotionally excited voters to discriminate or distinguish. To those who, like myself, believe that the great bulk of voters belong to this
moronic underworld, the success of the Huey Longs need
no other explanation. By nature endowed with the gifts
that appeal to the emotional and prejudiced masses, these
men need only the right opportunity and a certain political
shrewdness.
FRANK R. KENT: *Our Political Monstrosities,* 1933

An honest election, under democracy, is an act of inno-
cence which does not take place more than once in the
history of a given nation.
JOSÉ MARÍA GIL ROBLES: *Speech, Madrid,* 1933

. . . the system of building up, by corruption, political
machines dominated by a boss whom the corporations believe essential to them for corrupt purposes of their own,

134

is too deeply entrenched even yet in our national life. Every link in the chain that runs from the corporation desiring political favors down to the policeman on the beat levying his toll on the prostitute or the apple-seller is too strong to have been broken yet. [T. R.] Roosevelt was right. Big business does not want honest government, and so long as government is not honest, and the laws are not justly and impartially administered, every business man, even if he desires to be honest, finds himself caught in the system of great or petty graft and bribery.

JAMES TRUSLOW ADAMS: *The March of Democracy,* II, 1933

Politics unfortunately abounds in shams that must be treated reverentially by every politician who would succeed.

Ibid.

There is no more independence in politics than there is in jail.

WILL ROGERS (1879-1935)

I tell you folks, all politics is apple sauce.

WILL ROGERS

There are no friends at cards or world politics.

FINLEY PETER DUNNE (1867-1936)

The first need of human society is to be governed.

FREDERICK SCOTT OLIVER: *Politics and Politicians,* 1934

. . . politics cannot properly be regarded as a branch of virtuous conduct; for though the two things are often intertwined, each has its own separate root and stem.

Ibid.

Political power possesses a peculiar and indefinable integrating quality, important for the individual personality and for the social group of which he is a part. The concepts of order, of justice, of leadership, of responsibility, of trusteeship, of coordination, and of cooperation are rooted deep in the inner life of the individual and the association of individuals which we term society; and the adequate functioning of political power is essential to the fullest and richest development of the individual no less than of the group life.

CHARLES E. MERRIAM: *Political Power,* 1934

There are aspects of power which are not attractive but repulsive. There is a darker but none the less real side of behavior, a phase of authority hateful to many; to some indeed shamefulness appears as the typical power situation rather than the credenda and miranda. . . . We may note: 1. Violence, cruelty, terror, arrogance. 2. Hypocrisy, deceit, intrigue. 3. Corruption and privilege. 4. Inflexibility, stubbornness. 5. Backwardness, tardy adaptation to progress. 6. Indecision, impotence.

Ibid.

A smoothly functioning political order has little need of thought about propaganda among members of its own community. An ideology, once accepted, perpetuates itself with remarkable vitality. The individuals born into the

136

state direct some of their love toward the symbols which sustain the system: the common name, the common heroes, the common mission, the common demands. Some destructive tendencies are directed against rivals, traitors, heresies, and counterdemands. Individuals generate feelings of guilt in connection with the complex process of growing up; and some of this guilt is projected away from the individual and upon symbols of the collective enemies, which are treated as shameful violators of the mores. Personal weakness, too, is projected upon the world outside; after all, is not the enemy destined to defeat in our victory?

HAROLD D. LASSWELL: *Politics: Who Gets What, When, How?*, 1936

Political campaigns are designedly made into emotional orgies which endeavor to distract attention from the real issues involved, and they actually paralyze what slight powers of cerebration man can normally muster.

JAMES HARVEY ROBINSON (1863-1936): *The Human Comedy*, 1937

We will spend and spend, and tax and tax, and elect and elect.

Ascribed to HARRY L. HOPKINS: To Max Gordon at the Empire Race Track, Yonkers, New York, August, 1938

The Ohio Gang [of the Harding Administration] traded in liquor withdrawal permits, protection to bootleggers, appointments to office, illegal concessions, immunity from prosecution, pardons, paroles, privileges and general graft.

SAMUEL HOPKINS ADAMS: *Incredible Era*, 1939

137

Politics is the means by which the will of the few becomes the will of the many.

HOWARD KOCH and JOHN HUSTON: *In Time to Come*, I, 2, 1941

Politics is the art of preventing people from busying themselves with what is their own business.

PAUL VALÉRY: *Tel quel*, 1943

Politics is the gentle art of getting votes from the poor and campaign funds from the rich, by promising to protect each from the other.

OSCAR AMERINGER (1870-1943): *The American Guardian*

Each party steals so many articles of faith from the other, and the candidates spend so much time making each other's speeches, that by the time election day is past there is nothing much to do save turn the sitting rascals out and let a new gang in. This is not theoretical democracy, but it is actual democracy.

H. L. MENCKEN: *Generally Political*, 1944

... the public always tires of its messiahs, and soon or late invariably turns them out, whether they be good, which is uncommon, or bad, which is the rule.

Ibid.

... professional politicians seldom believe in reform, and almost never in the reforms they advocate. . . . Not half of the Senators and Congressmen who were lately supporting the New Deal really believed in it, or made any effort to conceal that fact behind the curtain.

Ibid.

The human race has never succeeded in fashioning a government that was even 20 per cent good. The effort is always a failure, here, there and everywhere. It is mankind's most gorgeous flop.

Ibid. (Cf. Plato)

Our system of checks and balances, the pride of our trusting hearts, is really not between the executive, the legislature and the judiciary, but between the people and the politicians of the country, which is to say, between its fools and its rogues. The people keep the politicians from stealing too much, and the politicians keep the people from getting too crazy.

Ibid.

... the people perform a valuable service every time they rise up for some possibly good but usually bad reason, and throw the politicians of a whole party out. It doesn't make much difference whether the victims are Democrats or Republicans, Liberals or Tories, mere pickpockets or downright burglars. The essential thing is they are thrown out. The experience chastens them, at least until they can get back.

Ibid.

A national campaign is better than the best circus ever heard of, with a mass baptism and a couple of hangings thrown in. It is better, even, than war.

Ibid.

Who gets what, when, how? [Cited as "a common definition of politics."]

> H. L. MENCKEN: *American Language*
> *Supplement I*, 283, 1945

What we need and what we want is to moralize politics, and not to politicise morals.

> K. R. POPPER: *The Open Society and Its*
> *Enemies*, 1945

The premises of politics lie in the conclusions of ethics.

> *Ibid.*

Class and group divisions based on property lie at the basis of modern governments; and politics and constitutional law are inevitably a reflex of these contending interests.

> CHARLES A. BEARD (1874-1948)

As yet no country has organized its government along scientific lines. Men have been ruled by god kings, priest kings and golden kings. They have been governed by consuls, kaisers, and commissars, and by princes, premiers, and presidents. Men have devised government by trial and error and their forms of government have been numberless. More than two thousand years ago Aristotle, with his students at the Lyceum, made a study of 158 political constitutions. It is a matter of rather recent history that the Dail Eireann made a study of constitutions when Ireland achieved her independence; yet the new government of

Ireland embraces the old and enduring psychological weaknesses.

C. S. BLUEMEL (M.A., M.D., F.A.C.P., M.R.C.S.):
War, Politics and Insanity, 1948

In our age there is no such thing as "keeping out of politics." All issues are political issues, and politics itself is a mass of lies, evasions, folly, hatred, and schizophrenia.

GEORGE ORWELL (1903-1950)

Democracy substitutes the election by the incompetent many for appointment by the corrupt few.

GEORGE BERNARD SHAW (1856-1950)

The opportunities for enrichment in Washington have come along in great variety. It is a general condition, not the isolated demoralization of one or two agencies, that confronts us. . . . When the lode at one agency plays out, another is discovered that takes its place. Tolerance and favoritism run through the capital like an underground stream, often out of sight but always within reach.

BLAIR BOLLES: *How to Get Rich in Washington,* 1952

Nowhere are prejudices more mistaken for truth, passion for reason, and invective for documentation than in politics. That is a realm, peopled only by villains or heroes, in which everything is black or white and gray is a forbidden color.

JOHN MASON BROWN: *Through These Men,* 1952

An empty stomach is not a good political adviser.

ALBERT EINSTEIN (1879-1955)

Since the birth of our nation, the "Big Fix" has been the curse of our party politics. The *Credit Mobilier* scandal under Grant, the Teapot Dome tragedy under Harding, the five-percenters and bribed tax collectors under Truman, are the recurring outbreaks of a chronic illness.

NEWBOLD MORRIS: *Let the Chips Fall,* 1955

In politics and in business one sees many a person who accepts democracy and freedom as permission to grab from and outwit other persons, maintaining that they are doing the admirable thing in achieving "success" for themselves in their field, despite the cost to others. . . .

LEON J. SAUL, M.D.: *The Hostile Mind,* 1956

. . . it is a paradox of a business civilization that there has been notably less political corruption in America than in many precapitalist societies such as in Asia, the Middle East, and South America, or even in some of the Latin societies of Europe . . . for those to whom money is all-important there are in America (as in no other culture) more direct channels open to the money-making energies. . . .

MAX LERNER: *America as a Civilization,* 1957

The mechanism of Communist power is perhaps the simplest which can be conceived, although it leads to the most refined tyranny and the most brutal exploitation. The simplicity of this mechanism originates from the fact that one party alone, the Communist Party, is the backbone of the entire political, economic, and ideological activity. The entire public life is at a standstill or moves ahead, falls behind or turns around according to what happens in the party forums.

Milovan Djilas: The New Class, 1957

The Communist revolution is the first in which the revolutionaries and their allies, particularly the authority-wielding group, survived the revolution.

Ibid., 28

Every revolution, and even every war, creates illusions and is conducted in the name of unrealizable ideals. During the struggle the ideals seem real enough for the combatants; by the end they often cease to exist. Not so in the case of a Communist revolution. Those who carry out the Communist revolution as well as those among the lower echelons persist in their illusions long after the armed struggle. Despite oppression, despotism, unconcealed confiscations, and privileges of the ruling echelons, some of the people—and especially the Communists—retain the illusions contained in their slogans.

Ibid., 30

In 1936, when the new Constitution was promulgated, Stalin announced that the "exploiting class" had ceased to exist. The capitalist and other classes of ancient origin had in fact been destroyed, but a new class, previously unknown to history, had been formed. . . . This new class, the bureaucracy, or more accurately the political bureaucracy, has all the characteristics of earlier ones as well as some new characteristics of its own.

Ibid., 38

143

The monopoly which the new class establishes in the name of the working class over the whole of society is, primarily, a monopoly over the working class itself.

Ibid., 42

The Communist political bureaucracy uses, enjoys, and disposes of nationalized property.

Ibid., 44

Politics is like a race horse. A good jockey must know how to fall with the least possible damage.

EDOUARD HERRIOT (1872-1957)

Not every one is attracted to politics. A recent survey by Professors Samuel J. Eldersveld and Daniel Katz of the University of Michigan shows this dramatically. These two scholars found that more than half the adults in Wayne County (Detroit), Michigan, thought that politics was dirty and dishonest. Nearly half the political volunteers and political workers in the county thought so, too.

DAVID BOTTER: *Politicians and What They Do,*
XVII, 1960

The price for which government is sold out in New York ranges from a handful of dollars to high political favors. The Special Unit found evidence of sales at all levels, ranging from the clerk who accepts $2 for filing an application out of turn, to the Commissioner who manipulates bidding procedures in order to favor a politically powerful contractor. Generally speaking the dollar corruption among City employees themselves exists on the lower levels. In the upper echelons, the corruption involves political power and influence with the indications being that if any money is paid it goes to political leaders instead of to officials themselves.

WHITNEY NORTH SEYMOUR, JR.: *Government for Sale;* Final Report of the Special Unit, New York State Commission of Investigation, July, 1961

Frequently they (lobbyists in the nineteenth century) appealed to the underpaid Congressmen with the offers of bribes; and frequently also, from contemporary accounts, they appealed to lonely Congressmen with the offer of women.

NEIL MACNEIL: *Forge of Democracy,* 1963

. . . the Southern Pacific Railroad, hired sitting members of the House like Oakes Ames of Massachusetts, who passed out valuable stocks to his fellow members "where it would do the most good."

Ibid.

The lobbyists, however, devised a far more subtle means of passing money to members of Congress than by ugly and obvious bribes. This was the technique of deliberately losing at cards to Congressmen, a technique used as late as the Harding administration in the 1920s.

Ibid.

Politics is dirty, Congress is undemocratic, our class leadership is inept.

DAVID T. BAZELON: *The Paper Economy,* 1963

It is ironic that the United States should have been founded by intellectuals, for throughout most of our political history, the intellectual has been for the most part either an outsider, a servant, or a scapegoat.

RICHARD HOFSTADTER: *Anti-Intellectualism in American Life,* 1963

Corruption is no stranger to Washington; it is a famous resident.

WALTER GOODMAN: *All Honorable Men,* 1963

For all the uproar that accompanied the tales of vicuna coats and cruises by yacht, of loans that were not paid back, hospitality that went unreciprocated and outside investments that impinged on inside duties, the past decade offers only pale additions to the flamboyant annals of public chicanery in America.

Ibid.

Neither politics nor revolution shows any mercy to the lives and fortunes of men.

SVETLANA ALLILUYEVA STALIN: *Twenty Letters to a Friend,* 1967

The people are no more capable of organizing and acting to attain and guard their general interests by sound political action than they are of achieving immortality by incantation and prayer. Unless saved by forces outside themselves they are perpetually doomed to be victims of their own ineptitude or of their shrewd exploiters.

FERDINAND LUNDBERG: *Scoundrels All,* 1968

Politics is the most practical of the arts. It is most concerned with "hard facts": For what facts are harder than

146

the facts of human interest and passion? Yet it is, and always has been, the most theoretical . . . conducted on the basis of some theory, theological or other, of authority and the obligation of obedience.

WILLIAM ERNEST HOCKING (1873-   )

A political war is one in which everyone shoots from the lip.

RAYMOND MOLEY (1886-   )

In politics where immediate success is attained by saying what people can be made to believe, rather than what is demonstrably true, accent is generally placed on the desirable rather than on the possible.

RAYMOND MOLEY

Before you can begin to think about politics at all, you have to abandon the notion that here is a war between good men and bad men.

WALTER LIPPMANN (1889-   )

Politics is a profession; a serious, complicated and, in its true sense, a noble one.

DWIGHT D. EISENHOWER (1890-   )

Politics is and has always been an imitation of war aimed at exorcising war.

MAX ASCOLI (1898-   )

Through politics, men can learn to use ballots instead of weapons.

MAX ASCOLI

Once politics enters, the entire edifice of an enterprise built upon expert skills becomes unsafe.

DAVID E. LILIENTHAL (1899-   )

Deriving from the cult of state, of party, of power, politics are always sacrificing the interests and aspirations of man for a multi-headed monster, for an idol.

IGNAZIO SILONE (1900-   )

In politics, familiarity doesn't breed contempt. It breeds votes.

PAUL LAZARSFELD (1901-   )

In politics, merit is rewarded by the possessor being raised, like a target, to a position to be fired at.

CHRISTIAN NEVELL BOVEE

Political platforms are for one party to stand on, and the other to jump on.

ARNOLD H. GLASOW

Fire, water, storms, robbers, rulers—these are the five great evils.

Burmese proverb

Office will show the man.

Greek proverb

Politics is a rotten egg; if broken open, it stinks.

Russian proverb

Common American Political Sayings

A political campaign is a combination of mud, threats and smears.

A political campaign starts when a politician stops work and goes about making speeches about all the work he intends to do.

A political convention is an assembly at which factions speak louder than wards and districts.

A political machine is a united minority working against a divided majority.

A political platform is like the platform of a trolley car—not meant to stand on but just to get in on.

Political promises go in one year and out the other.

"Political economy" is a phrase consisting of two incompatible words.

Politics consists of one gang trying to get into office and another trying to stay in.

Politics estranges strange bedfellows.

Politics estranges political bedfellows.

Politics makes strange bedfellows stranger.

Politics makes strange bedfellows, but they soon get accustomed to the common bunk.

Politics is the art of looking for trouble, finding it everywhere, diagnosing it incorrectly and applying the wrong remedies.

Politics is a game in which some men are self-made but most are machine-made.

Politics is the science of who gets what—and how!

Politics is a tug of war between people who want to get in and people who don't want to get out.

In politics be sure you're "in right," then grab.

In politics people work hard to get a job and do little after they get it.

Liberty in politics is a case of taking liberties with right and truth.

Strange bedfellows make strange politics.

Voters are people who have the God-given right to decide who will waste their money for them.

Epilogue

After all these varied comments about politicians and politics, most of them adverse, the reader will be apt either to throw up his hands and mutter that we must do the best we can with the means at hand or to ask what is proposed as a way out of the obvious impasse. No better suggestion has been made, it seems to me, than Plato's of placing men of superior knowledge and discernment in charge of public affairs. If men of superior knowledge cannot turn out a better performance than the present sodden, disorientedly aggressive fly-by-nights in politics, then there is, clearly, no hope for saving or advancing civilization. Placing men of known superior knowledge in office is the one remedy that has never been applied anywhere.

How would one place men of superior knowledge in office? And what would constitute their superior knowledge?

There would, first, need to be constitutional eligibility rules for qualified men. Nobody deemed unqualified would be allowed to stand for office.

What would constitute a qualified man? A political officer, manifestly, requires many qualities of character, and of these we need not speak here. But a preliminary qualification in the search for superior men would be that they hold first-class university degrees or show by examination an equivalent mastery of relevant subject matter. What constitutes a first-class university degree and what subject matter would underlie its possession can be left to appropriate definition. Were these immediate practical questions I would have my own suggestions to offer.

A psychiatrist, C. S. Bluemel, has suggested that the teachers of those who may become officeholders also be required to record their opinions of their students' emotional stability. Supplementing such a provision there might be the requirement that psychiatrists pass on the emotional character of all persons eligible to enter the pool of prospective officeholders, just as they now pass on prospective members of the armed forces. Adverse findings with respect to the emotional composition of a prospective officeholder, no matter how learned he was, would automatically keep him out of the pool.

Once the pool was established it would be the rule that all officeholders must be chosen from it. Anyone not in the pool would be ineligible to hold office. While all those persons brought into the pool by these means would be no absolute guarantee of political salvation for society, there would at least be some guarantee against the presence of the egregiously ignorant, the irresponsible, and the emotionally disturbed, each prominently present in politics at all times down through history. The worst that might be feared is that some members in the reserve pool of prospective officeholders would deteriorate, an eventuality that can hardly be guarded against. Those who take a pessimistic view of history can be reassured that the pool might produce some undesirable cases. But the probability would be greatly reduced. In any event, the crop of officeholders would be no worse than at present.

How would officeholders be chosen from among the eligibles?

They would, as at present under various systems, either be coopted or elected.

However, if they are chosen in a popular electoral system, there could be a further guarding against bad choices by an unevenly informed electorate through the weighting of the vote of the electorate according to the formal educational attainments of each member of the electorate. What I mean here is simply that there be some system of popular voting about as follows: One vote for every citizen, two votes for all citizens who had completed elementary school, four votes for all who had completed high school, and sixteen votes for all who had completed a nonvocational course of study in an accredited college.

As under present conditions in the United States educated people tend to concentrate in a few metropolitan regions, leaving vast stretches of the country to woefully uninformed leadership, there would need to be changes in present residency requirements so that, as in England, candidates need not be residents of the states and regions that returned them to office. Qualified candidates might stand for office anywhere, unqualified persons nowhere.

Skeptics will smile at the simple naivete of my suggestions. Yet this is the kind of system we have for licensing physicians and surgeons and, in the more advanced jurisdictions, lawyers and engineers. None of these is allowed to practice without a public license which requires a course of formal learning that insures some modicum of scrupulosity in the practitioner. And the function of the political officeholder, judge, and lawmaker is at least as important as any of these. In a general way it is more important.

If physicians were selected in the way our officeholders are selected, anyone might practice medicine who could command sufficient votes from an uninformed, excited populace. Quacks would predominate in medicine, as they now do in politics.

Yet, it will be urged, even if it is conceded that I have suggested a superior way of staffing government, it would be impossible under the existing constitution to institute such sweeping reforms. For the very provisions of the present constitution relating to changes make any fundamental changes in effect impossible short of revolution. The existing political managers would not be likely to yield their power through argument, petition, or supplication for a better system.

While this is no doubt true, it must be remembered I am not advancing these proposals as an immediately practical matter but simply to show that, intellectually, the problem is solvable. And it is an important problem; for the fundamental difficulties of the nation, and of the world, are not economic (as often claimed) but are political. On the important side of production, the economic problem has been technically solved; there is enough for everybody. This is generally conceded.

It is in the distribution of what is produced that the problem lies, and the distribution is governed by rules derived solely from the political process. Those rules will not soon be changed by persons chosen through the existing political process, which has quite clearly broken down into a private arrangement of the big proprietors and their henchmen. To expect the beneficiaries of a defective system of choosing lawmakers and executives to yield gracefully to a new and better order that would install better lawmakers, judges, and executive officers is to expect the impossible.

Whether the problem is ever solved in practice as it has been intellectually must be left to history. It will hardly be solved in practice by the so-called orderly parliamentary processes, which are simply the processes of self-serving cloakroom intrigue on the part of bought politicos.

What, it may be asked, would be gained by having more intelligent and more informed men throughout the public offices? As I see it, we would have more intelligent and more informed public policies. Just what those policies might be we do not know; for they would have to be developed in intelligent and informed debate instead of, as in the present system, by means of behind-the-scenes horse trading and backscratching.

Unless intelligence and knowledge are inferior guides, a system that placed into office more intelligent and more informed men ought to produce superior public policies. To believe otherwise is to turn one's back on intelligence and knowledge in favor of mysticism and obscurantism, which are the guiding lights of the present misnamed democratic system.

What the world has, as a consequence of the types placed in office, is a system of pretty uniformly sinister governments, ruled predominantly by Mafian types. While I would not regard the governments of Canada, Iceland, and the Scandinavian countries as particularly sinister, from there on they can be shown to increase in ominousness by degrees from the smaller to the larger. They are all, in fact, universally recognized as sinister by government leaders, who self-servingly except only their own jurisdictions from the designation.

In this matter I would defer collectively to all the leading politicians. While giving full force and credit to what American and British politicians say about the Moscow and Peking regimes and personnel, I give equal weight to what the Moscow and Peking practitioners say about their western colleagues. And not only is the sinister thrust of the various regimes directed outward; it is directed inward as well, at the majority of the home populations.

For Americans, among the most naive politically in the world, such will appear to be a strange and even aberrant judgment. Americans are so habituated to looking with distrust at foreigners that it will hardly be a surprising notion to them that the politicians of Paris, Berlin, Tokyo, Peking, and Moscow (to mention only a few centers of iniquity) are up to no good. That their own political leaders are up to as much devilment at home and abroad is a more difficult notion for many to swallow. That the leaders of the Republican and Democratic Parties may be more inimical to general American well being than Leonid

156

Breszhnev, Mao Tse Tung, or Charles de Gaulle (because they are closer and command more misplaced confidence) is a notion that few can be expected to agree with in the United States. Yet I believe it to be painfully true.

For it is the inept, insufficiently instructed leaderships of all nations that are the prime cause of political debacle in the home countries. It is to a long line of unwarrantably supercilious British prime ministers and cabinets that we must look for the causes of the abrupt shrinkage of the recently vaunted British Empire rather than to the machinations of the Kaiser, Stalin, and Hitler.

Naturally, as long as people are willing to put up with the ineptitude of the catch-as-catch-can politicians, sobering but avoidable events will continue to take place, affecting all countries. Politics will remain an untended infection. One civilization after the other will, as hitherto, continue to decline and fall.

Index

159

160

161